UP: FROM WHERE WE'VE COME

Copyright © 2015 by Charles W. Wright

Library of Congress Control Number:

PCN Number   2015918563

To order additional copies of this book, contact:

www.expressyourself.net

TABLE OF CONTENTS

A SPECIAL THANKS TO ...

My Brother Frankie D., My son Dennis Wright and his wife Rose, My daughter Shaloa Robinson, My son in-law Bo Robinson, My grandkids Cameron & Zaria Robinson, Tianna & D.J, The entire Wright family, The Robinson family, Mark Dubuclet (art director & production assistant, Ronald Benjamin (assistant director), Roland Bynum, Little Richard Penniman, Congress Lady Maxine Waters, Scott Galloway (Editing), Barbara Morrison & Gary, Phil Brown, Frank Trenado (photographer), Eva C. Wright (deceased), Vernice, Akeisa & Precillia Smith, Marcella Hall, Paulette Hawkins, Joyce Logan, Jai' Saint Laurent (Publicist), Chip Schutzman (Social media), Ryan Schmitt & Anthony Gibson of Verve Mgmt., G-Mack, Thereasa Lee, Peaches and Precillia.

REVIEW

It gives me great pleasure to Express how I feel after reading Up: From Where We've Come" by my friend Charles Wright. Even though I have known Charles for more than forty years, this first installment of his life I found to be very thought provoking and touching. One of the most powerful components of this book is his portrayal of the relationship of the sharecropper, and that of an African-American family during the 30s and 40s here in the United States. The enduring relationship that his mother and father had as parents raising twelve children in the south, shows that very important connection between children and their parents prior to the modern day civil rights movement in the south.

I found that reading this book kept me engrossed and tied very closely to Charles and his sharecropping family. It is heartbreaking, intriguing, and in many instances when I read how his father and mother as sharecroppers were treated by the whites in the South during the 40s, demonstrated the power of the African American family, who survived through their religious and spiritual beliefs. Also, when I read how his brother McClain accidentally shot their friend Bill Williams I was drawn in as if I was there myself. What is amazing is the recollection that Charles has about the many events that took place while he was a little boy. I felt that many times his family, and many of the African-Americans sharecroppers were terrorized by the white land owners during that time, and were cheated beyond belief, and just blatantly treated as if they were slaves.

Charles indicates that he embellishes some of the events during this journey; however this does not take away from the authenticity of the book. I have known Charles for more than 40 years, and yet I feel like most of you that before you read his memoirs that we tend to see entertainers as one who has done music all their life, and we find that this is not true in his book "Up From Where We've Come."

I find it interesting that Mr. Wright's use of the conjunction "We've for we have to include all of us in his personal journey and enlightenment. This is not just a personal memoir about himself, it's about all of us who lived during that time frame from the 30s, 40s and 50s, and especially in the south if you were sharecropper. If your family were sharecroppers you endured this kind of mistreatment from the white society, and more importantly you were not expected to succeed beyond that reality. The fact that Charles Wright did come from a southern sharecropping slave mentality environment, and to succeed in life as he did to become a world renown musician says a lot about the endurance of the African-American families in this country.

Charles, his brothers, his sisters, his parents, and many like him, were not supposed to succeed. But, on the contrary, with the timeline of post-depression, his mother and father having ten children, and living in conditions that were not conducive for success, he tells us a lot about the African-American experience through the book, and the eyes, and the spirit, and the soul of Mr. Charles Wright.

You see, we all come from somewhere, and Charles Wright gets it right in this tell all memoir. You can take the man out of the country, but you can't take the country out of the man. A must read for all who understand what *it means to "Express Yourself."*

Roland Bynum

This Machine has taken the place of at least 10,000 hands...

14

PREFACE

This is my story and most of it is one hundred percent true. I started writing this story over forty years ago, which is at least twice as long as the content herewith. And though I tried I soon came to realize that I could not cram my life story into a single volume. I therefore decided to dice it up into at least two or three, and maybe even four separate parts.

It seems some people are disappointed when I mention that I wrote a book, which has little to do with my musical career. Yet as anyone can so plainly see there is much more to my life than the fact that I chose to play music as a livelihood.

My next book will deal with my middle and high school years, my musical beginnings and, hopefully, my entire career, which most people are looking forward to.

There are parts in this book that are embellished such as conversations I wasn't privy to and situations I did not personally witness. It is in these situations that I enjoyed the freedom to express myself by using my vivid imagination to add a little color to my storyline. For example; I did witness most of my father's confrontations with his sharecropping partners. Practically everything I accuse them of is true. However, I was not in the car with my parents on that moonlit night when they were hot and bothered, and cannot be certain that conversation took place. Yet, I had fun writing this particular chapter because though they sired ten children in that little shack we lived in, never once did I hear the slightest indication that they were making babies...which is more than I could ever attest to!

Some may consider these chapters a vital part of America's history, which has yet to be told in this particular fashion. Others may think that I am simply spinning yarns concerning my childhood. Yet I hope that at least some of you will gain a clearer understanding of how awfully close the relationship between sharecropping and slavery had become, and the plight of a people that have constantly been thrown from the skillet into the frying pan - on this side of the planet, as well as places beyond our shores.

As you can see there is much more to my life than me choosing music as my livelihood. I sincerely hope you get half as much out of reading these pages as I did writing them. It was a thrill to share my saga with the world. By doing so, a great weight has been lifted off of my shoulders.

We'll all come to the logical conclusion someday that we are all God's children and that we must ultimately learn to live together. Hopefully through an alternative train of thought, future generations will venture to make the world a better place where mankind will finally explore a better way of life.

God bless you, *Charles Wright*

CHAPTER 1 "IMAGES I RECALL"

For those of you that don't know, I wrote a book and it's about my life. And believe it or not, it started three months before I was born.

I explained this to my parents, who couldn't understand how I experienced such a thing three months before I was born. But I remember someone knocking on our door to tell my mother that my grandfather got killed while walking up the railroad tracks, a box of groceries on his head. So as I was trying to explain, I remembered what we had to eat that day. We had baked yams.

"Alright" she said, "So how'd your mama cook them yams honey?" She thought she had me cornered. "I bet you he won't be guessing up on that one anytime soon," she told my father.

"In the fireplace," I said to her surprise because that's where she had cooked them. She hadn't baked yams that way since my grandfather died because she didn't want to remind my father of the incident. . But as I tried to explain, my father who threatened to whip me shut me down.

In those days I was my father's biggest fan, who followed him every place he went, mimicked his every move, and was his greatest helper when he had work to do around the shack.

I remember one day he looked down upon me and said, "Boy, you're such a good worker. And I know you won't be like them no account brothers of yours, will you?"

"Oh, no sir," I said, not that I knew what he was talking about. My brothers, Grady and James Lee, weren't really lazy. They just didn't like picking and chopping cotton sunup 'til sundown - WITHOUT ANY PAY! However, this is something my father had done for as long as he could remember.

That was also the day he pulled this thing out and handed it to me.

It was a brand new axe handle, shining against the mid-day sun.

"I need you to help me fix this axe," he said as he balanced it on a rickety table. So he took the metal part of this apparatus and applied it to the other end of the stick, then hit the thing with a hammer, which seemed to jar my hands to bits. So I jumped back and said, "Oh, no!" That's when I saw this look in his eyes, as if he thought I wasn't up to the task. But as soon as my hand cooled down, I grabbed the thing again. And this time when he hit it, the metal part flipped then came down and landed dead in the middle of my foot, practically cutting it in two! I looked at my foot. It looked normal, so I picked it up and skipped across the porch on my other foot. Then I turned around and on the way back, took another look at my foot but saw something different this time. Clearly, I saw the pink interior of my bone! And oh, my God, did I let out a scream... the loudest one my lungs could expel.

"Oh, my God," said my father who ran back into the shack and returned with a raggedy sheet and a lamp dripping kerosene! "What have I done," he said? So he
18

took my foot and poured kerosene all over it after which he tied it up real tight. He then took me in his arms, and rocked me back and forth. "There-there now," he said. "You're your daddy's special baby boy. I know you know that now don't you? You're your daddy's special baby boy."

He then looked to the sky as he wondered what my mother would say when she returned.

Grady had hooked the wagon up to take my mother to the store. "Oh, my God," she said when they returned! "I oughta let you babysit more often. So how'd you get this one to fall asleep in the middle of the day?"

My daddy didn't say a word. He just stood there dumbfounded.

"Well, how'd you do it?"

"I don't want you to go getting all upset for nothing," sweat dripping from his brow. "But this boy was helping me do something today and he kinda got hurt."

"Kinda got hurt?"

"Yeah, his foot kinda got hurt."

"So what do you mean kinda got hurt?"

"The boy was helping me and we had a stupid ole' accident, Magnolia, and he kinda got his foot hurt."

My mother, suddenly angry, started exuding these invisible things, which went a-bouncing off the walls

19

and sticking into my father like pins and needles.

She grabbed my foot and as she was beginning to unwrap` it, "But Magnolia," said my father, "I done told you I fixed it up already. You gonna mess up everything!"

"Yeah I know you done fixed it all right. I'm just trying to see how much fixing you done-done here," she said as she continued to

unwrap my foot. "Oh, my God!" she exclaimed, "What's this? So much blood!"

She unwrapped some more until she could see my wound. "OH, MY GOD," she shouted! "What have you done, Edmond? Is you trying to kill this child? Go get that doctor! Go get Doc Rainey! Hurry up and go get Doc Rainey!"

I'd never seen my dad in such a frantic state. He rushed into the little hallway, snatched his hat from a nail and out the door he went toward Mattson to get Doc Rainey.

CHAPTER 2   "DOC RAINEY"

Doc Rainey was a freckle-faced white man with red hair who wore a southern gentleman's hat, a paisley shirt and creamy white pants. He wobbled as he walked into the shack ahead of my father.

Now I'd seen Doc Rainey passing the shack many times in his light blue Dodge Sedan. In fact, only a few days before as Frankie D and I were playing at the edge of the road, he passed us by and we couldn't help but notice how he swerved a few hundred feet beyond the shack. So when the dust settled, Frankie D and I held inspection only to discover a snake, twisting and turning in agony, with tread marks across its back.

Now, I couldn't read or write at the time but I figured anyone who'd do something like that was wrong. And though it may have been called for, in my mind it seemed quite unnecessary. I didn't particularly like Doc Rainey so I was trying to get away from him as he entered the door with a black satchel in his hand.

"Don't let him touch me," I begged. "Mama, please don't let him touch me!"

"But the doctor came all this way to help us out," said my mother, "so please, Honey, do your best to cooperate, okay?"

The doctor was a gentle man and especially knew how to deal with children. He went into his bag and pulled out this little teddy bear. He handed it down to me but I didn't want anything to do with it. Everything was fine until he took this long-stemmed swab and dipped it into a reddened solution. Then he took the shit and dripped it down in my wound. Now if you thought I'd screamed before, I can almost guarantee my grandparents down the road must've thought someone was killing me! I screamed so loud until my father headed for the doorway and wasn't seen until I woke up the next day to a host of birds in a tree outside my window.

CHAPTER 3   "WHOSE PIES"

My father always quoted the Bible. Yet the phrase 'Yield not to temptation' must have eluded me and Frankie D., especially when it came to Mom's delectable desserts. She'd often cook them, forget and leave them on top of the stove - in which case we'd have a field day of our own! She cooked peach cobblers, blackberry cobblers, apple and sweet potato pies or sometimes a couple of juicy yams. So, expecting a delicious treat after a hard day's work, the field hands often celebrated in disappointment. Yet they'd have some fun at the expense of our overstuffed butts.

I remember one night my mother spoke up slightly after her anger subsided, "Who," she asked, "ate my pies while I was breaking my back in the cotton patch?" All the while, she's looking at me.

With a pouting expression, I looked her dead in the eye and said, "Them wuz my pies!" To which my siblings all burst out laughing. My father, meanwhile, was trying to hold on to his emotions - a task which he'd find difficult to perform. So I turned and looked at Frankie D who was frightened out of his wits. The rest of them turned their attention towards Frankie D. as well, his legs wobbling as urine trickled down his thigh.

"He did it," said Frankie D. "He ate 'em all up by his self!"

"Ah ha," said Edna Rea, the girl two years older than me. "What'd I say? Just look at 'em - he's guilty all right!"

"Was you up here at the house or were you out there in

24

the cotton patch with the rest of us," asked my daddy?

"Uh-uh, no, uh-uh...I mean, yes, sir."

"Then I suggest you stay in your place then," said my father.

Edna Rea settled back down and stuck her thumb into her mouth.

Slapping her hand now with a belt taken from Dad's Sunday trousers, Mom asked, "Do you know how hard I worked on them pies? And just like that," said Mom snapping her finger, "you went and under-minded everything I'd set out to do." She then stopped slapping her hand but just long enough to dawn her face with graveness. "Come on over here," she said. "Bring your narrow tail over here."

So I inched my way towards my mother's outstretched hand, rubbing my buttocks. The consequences of what we'd done were frightening but I was wondering why I was being singled out.

"Didn't I tell you to come over here, boy, and tell me whose pies you ate?"

"My pies," I repeated!

"Well, come on over here and tell me that!"

Now the sweet aroma of them pies actually compelled me to feel as though they deserved my personal attention. Yet Frankie D. had indulged himself deeper than I had, so why wasn't he being whipped?

My mother must have sensed my anxiety. "Don't worry about Frankie D.," she said, "I'm gonna tear into his butt no sooner than I get through with you! But right now, I want you to come over here and tell me whose pies them was you ate."

"Mine," I insisted.

"Well c'mon over here then," said Mom.

But upon hearing his name, Frankie D. started wailing, "I didn't do nothing", he said. "C.W. - he ate 'em all up by his self!"

But the boy's lying and I'm wondering why no one realizes how Frankie D. can out-eat practically everyone in the family. So reflecting through my tears, I remembered the day our Aunt Nancy babysat us and Frankie D. ate eight slices of toast in a single sitting! I protested when he asked for the ninth slice but my aunt, who was a spoiler, gave it to him anyway. His eyes were bigger than his stomach so he left most of it in the dirt where we were playing. A hoard of ants hauled it away, a crumb at a time.

By the time I inched my way into my mom's reach, most of my siblings' laughter had abated and I think they were pulling for me. I believe they appreciated my tenacity... all except for Edna Rea and Jessie Mae, the two girls older than me, neither of whom appreciated my audacity.

Jessie Mae was the skinniest of us all but picked cotton like an animated machine. She could pick more than anyone in the family, including my mother and father. She'd picked more than 250 pounds so, as far as she was concerned, no one deserved those pies more than she. Besides, this little fiasco had stretched far beyond her ability to withstand.

No sooner than Mom started whipping me, Jessie Mae's eyes lit up with sheer indulgence.

"Whose pies," asked my mom? "Did you cook any pies off up in here?"

"No ma'am!"

"Then whose pies?"

"My pies!"
"What?!"

Now my mama's whippings actually could've been dull and ineffective. But her booty thrashing along with her tongue-lashings turned the situation into a dramatic affair. 'Cause she always whipped you dead-on the word.

"I asked you whose PIES wuz them you ate?"

"My pies!"

"WHAT? Boy, you must be out of your mind!"

Finally when she turned me a loose, my butt was burning like wildfire! But the shrillness of my voice

27

must've irritated my father's sensitive eardrums.

"Boy," he said, "if you don't shut it down, I'm gonna tear into your butt myself!"

So I lay down on the floor and I stuck my thumb into my mouth but made the mistake of looking up. Jessie Mae, who was seated on my father's lap, had her lips stretched all the way back and her tongue sticking out, making the most hideous face imaginable.

So I started to cry all over again.

"Magnolia," gruffed my father, "give me that strap! If you want something to cry about, I'll really give you something to cry about!"

So I laid back down and stuck my thumb back in my mouth, but this time she made and even uglier face. So I simply lay there trading ugly faces with Jessie Mae until I drifted off to sleep.

CHAPTER 4   "OLD MAN MILES"

The young rooster, who had the accuracy of a thousand timepieces, climbed atop his chicken's coop and let out a powerful crow, waking every creature within the sound of his voice. And for the Wright children, except Jessie Mae, his crow was a precursor to yet another dismal day. So while crawling out of bed, Grady grumbled, "That 'ole rooster. Next thing you know the old man's gonna be coming in here raising hell, too."

James Lee, the next younger boy, was lying in a puddle of urine and was afraid to move. 'God forbid,' he thought, 'his father should get a whiff of their mattress before they headed off to work.'

Soon afterwards, my father entered the room followed by the scent of cured bacon. Conducting his usual routine, "It's time to rise and shine," he said. "So everyone up and at 'em. We've got work to do!" Then after a hearty breakfast of fluffy biscuits, sorghum molasses, bacon and eggs and a glass of milk, my sister Jessie Mae led the family off into a field of whiteness.

Later on, Frankie D. and I played with makeshift toys. I ushered a bicycle rim along while Frankie D. manipulated this crane-like thing the two of us had put together. I eventually looked up and saw a cloud of dust. So we ran up on the porch and waited for a car to pass, but the car drove up and stopped abruptly! There was an old white man inside beckoning us to come closer. The first thing I noticed was the tobacco stains running down the driver's side door which apparently had been oozing down for quite some time.

The old man's dagger blue eyes seemed to penetrate to the core as he peered down upon us.

"Where," he asked, "is that no account father of yours?"

I pointed into the distance and said, "Out there in the cotton patch."

"I know he's in the cotton patch, tar baby, but which way did he go when he left here?"

I pointed towards the far twenties. He didn't say another word. He simply stuck his foot in the tank. His rear wheels went a-spinning and a-spinning, faster than the mass of metal could move. He was throwing rocks and dirt everywhere until the metal caught up with the wheels, which doused Frankie D. and I with gravel and dust. We simply covered our eyes after which we went back up on the porch and snuggled up against one another.

Only moments later, we heard the car humming as it came back towards us, dashing through the corn patch and scattering chickens into all directions. My father was in the car this time and it seemed like he was trying to tell us something, his head all out the window. But the only thing we understood due to the driver's recklessness was, "I'll be back soon!"

And just as promised, my father returned driving the

most beautiful car, which shone against the mid-day sun. It had the strangest antennae which curled from just above the windshield all the way to the back of the car's canopy. With his chest protruded, he swung the rear door open and said, "Just jump right on in." So with thundering hearts, Frankie D. and I climbed into the rear seat.

We'd seen countless cars pass the shack but never dreamt of riding in one. And unlike Mr. Miles, my father drove cautiously up the bumpy dirt road. The scent of the car's felt interior was so intriguing. Frankie D. and I were practically in seventh heaven as he drove into the prolific cotton patch. We were so excited we actually didn't notice what was going on out there until we saw the rest of the family shedding their sacks and coming a-rushing in our direction. Even my mom was walking faster than usual. "Look!" said Frankie D. "There's mama `nem!"

My daddy was happier that day than I'd ever seen him before or since. "Come on," he said! "We're about to take a spin around the countryside!" And once seated, my mother was beaming like a star and looking up at my father with a proud expression. "So, how do you like it," he asked?

"Oh honey, it's the most beautiful thing I ever seen!" Yet, she added, "I hope that old man don't take advantage of us for it, though."

After thinking about it, "Aw come on," said my father. "Don't go spoiling it already. At least give it a chance, o.k."

"Okay," said mom, "but don't forget you've been warned."

So after we all crowded in, my father took off and drove through the countryside until we came up on Highway 49. On the side of the road there was a sign that read Clarksdale 9 miles. So, "do you think we ought to try it," asked my father?

But "Hell no," said mother! "Just look at us! We look like a bunch of raggedy fee larks! Besides, you ain't even got no driving license."

"I know that and you know it. But do they know?"

"Irregardless," said my mom, "you ain't getting me and my chillun locked up in that Comma County jail!" Meanwhile she poked my father in the side with her elbow. "Look at that ole' ugly man over there," she said, "looking at us like we done stole something!"

There was an old white fellow on the opposite side of the highway standing by a T-model Ford. He was looking at my dad like he wanted to kill him dead on-the-spot!

"Aw, shucks," said Dad! "Ain't no sense in asking for trouble, now is it?" So he turned the car around and took us all back to where he'd picked us up, in the first place.

CHAPTER 5 "TO THE EDGE OF MYSELF"

As the majestic Chevrolet stirred the gravel road, my brothers McClain, Grady, James Lee, Frankie D. and me, and my sisters Jessie Mae and Edna Rea were all packed in the back seat like sardines. Mom and my oldest sister Inez, who wore pink and blue berets, sat in the front seat. And my mother was holding my baby sister Dorothy Jean. I was seated directly behind my father wondering why the moon seemed to be moving right along with the car. Yet every time we stopped, the moon stopped right along with us. And since I'd never been in a car at night, this was quite a puzzling situation.

There were six-dozen eggs on the floorboard beneath my mother's feet, which my parents hoped to sell once we reached the city limits. She'd accidently cracked several while situating the baby's bag on the floor. And for some reason, my father decided to eat one of the things raw. We watched as he finished cracking it on the steering wheel and applauded him as the slimy substance oozed down into his throat. "Auhhhgh," we said as he was gulping it down!

When finally we reached the highway, my father stuck his foot in the tank and we were off at 50 miles an hour. None of the younger children had ventured so far from home or traveled so fast. And as vehicles passed by in the opposite direction, the augmented sound of their approach and the swishing sound as they became parallel was blowing each and every one of our minds. All of us sat straight up in our seats, our eyes and mouths wide open with awesome expressions as our heads turned like frequently used doorknobs. Finally when we reached the edge of town, my father stopped in the middle of the highway, after which I asked, "Is this where we supposed to get out?"

"Why, no," said my dad with a hearty chuckle.

"Well, why did you stop?"

"For that light up there," he said. "It's red. See it?"

"No, sir."

"Well then! Jump on over into the front seat." So I climbed over the seat but by then it was green. "You see that light up yonder," he repeated? "It's green now."

"Oh, I see. But what made you stop?"

"So the cars going across that way they get a chance to go. And then we get another chance to go." I had never seen so many roads crossing one another.

So I didn't quite understand but my mom said, "Just shut up and enjoy the ride, o.k." Which was fine with my father since all he wanted was for me to get up into the front seat next to him anyway.

CHAPTER 6   "CLARKSDALE"

Clarksdale was the most exciting thing we'd ever experienced, especially for my younger sisters and brothers and me. We'd never seen an electric light before yet there were neon signs flashing on and off in every direction. My father's car was one among many slowly cruising the promenade. And there were hoards of people on the sidewalks who appeared to be having lots of fun! Mannequins in the storefront windows wore clothes like we'd never seen. And the policemen in the intersections waved their arms in a symmetrical motion. Oh, my God were we excited! Even my oldest sister Inez, who'd always been able to control her emotions - her eyes were about to pop out of her head.

My father, who glanced periodically at my mother, was getting a kick out of seeing her enjoy herself as she sat there, her head drifting from one side to the other. I turned to see how everyone else was doing and Frankie D.'s bottom lip was about to touch the floor. I was not that much better off myself.

"Umh-Umh-UMH," said my daddy every once in awhile. "This is really something! Lord, Lord, Lord this is really something," he exclaimed!

Eventually we passed a motion picture theater, which seemed bigger than life itself. We'd never seen anything like it. It had lights flowing out of one wall then around the triangular marquis and back into the opposite wall. And the popcorn... the popcorn smelled so good it set that building apart from all the other ones on the

36

promenade. And no sooner than we'd passed it, my sister Jessie Mae - whose head was all the way out the window - let out a blood-curdling scream which shocked us all back into reality.

My father's automatic reflexes took over so he slammed down on his brakes. But thanks to the fact that he knew whose scream it was - and why she was screaming - he took his foot off in time to avoid an accident. He'd seen Sterling through the corner of his eye. And there he was... a black man about 5 feet 10 inches tall, weighing approximately 160 pounds, who'd argue a barber down due the fact that his head was no bigger than the average man's fist. He therefore refused to pay more than 25 cent for a haircut.

"Oh, my God," screamed Edna Rea, "look a there Mama! That man... ain't got no head!" And suddenly, our hearts and minds were engrossed in anxiety. Sterling's eyes, due mostly to his larger than usual eyebrows, appeared unusually close to one another as he keyed in on Jessie Mae, who was responsible for the scream. He was giving her a negative vibe. I guess my sister's scream caused him to blink faster than usual. But it was my mother who gallantly saved the day. "Aw, honey," she said. "That ain't nothing but ole' Sterling Frackus. He's been standing there for years on end." And in the final analysis, Sterling mustered up enough sporting blood to wink at Jessie Mae before he went back to scanning his usual environment.

CHAPTER 7 "WOLFE & WOLFE"

My father eventually found a parking space and instructed Frankie D. and me to get out and go with him. So he took us by the hand and into the exuberant crowd. And though we had no idea of where he was taking us, we were nevertheless exhilarated. We eventually strolled into this sweet smelling place, which was the first ice cream parlor Frankie D. and I ever experienced. There was a white lady and three young girls, presumably her daughters, behind the counter serving soft-serve ice cream. My dad had already sent James Lee and Grady to the theater to purchase popcorn. So he handed me two cones and handed Frankie D. two while telling us, "Y'all take these to your mama and come back for more." But that's when we realized how difficult it was to navigate the Promenade. There were many people - seemed like thousands - going back and forth in both directions.

First thing I saw were these two little black girls about 10 or 11 years-old. One looked at me and licked her lips then said, "Look at that old greedy boy over there? He's got to have two cones all by his greedy ass self!" Finally when we reached the car, ice cream was dripping all over the place, so we handed the cones to our mother who distributed them among the rest. Then we dashed back on to the Promenade and re-entered the parlor where my father handed us two more cones each, "One of these is for you," he said, "so take the others and give them to your mother." He had a handful of cones himself and when we returned, he instructed me to get back into the back seat where everyone was crunching on popcorn or licking on ice cream.

My brother James Lee seemed to be enjoying his more than the rest. He'd licked the thing then looked at it in detail and said, "Boy, oh boy, this is some good stuff!"

"Man, oh man," said my brother Grady, "I could eat this seven days a week and twice on Sundays!" After which we all burst out laughing.

We then got lost in the confections. Forgot all about those fancy neon signs, at least for the time being. My father cautioned us not to get ice cream on his felt interior. We eventually became so engrossed in our taste buds until all else was reduced to a mere background noise. And before we knew it, my father had crossed over the Sunflower River and beneath the tunnel of the railroad viaduct. We had never been into a tunnel before. So my father, he blew his horn off in the tunnel, and Jesus Christ! I must have thought I'd died and went to Heaven. I'd never heard anything like the echo in that tunnel. I don't know why but I stuck my head out the window and screamed as loud as I possibly could.

But no sooner than my father realized whose squeaky voice it was, "Boy get your nappy head back in this car before I take my belt off and wear your tail out with it!" I'd made my hero angry and suddenly felt as though I'd completely lost my energy. So I leaned my head up against the felt door. And as we came up out of the tunnel, I saw this purple neon sign flashing on and off in two to three second intervals. All it said was Wolfe &

39

Wolfe, Wolfe & Wolfe, WOLFE & WOLFE!!!

Wolfe & Wolfe was one of the two funeral parlors in Comma County, each of which had two hearses. The Wolfe brothers had both a black and a green hearse. I had seen that green hearse. The first time I saw it was the day old man Williams died, as it crept up the gravel road en route to his shack. They had this long-headed man...this undertaker named Booker T. He always drove that green hearse. I'll never forget Booker T... that loooong-headed man in that green hearse.

CHAPTER 8 "BIG LEO CLARK"

Leo's duties were to keep the store clean, pump gasoline and deliver groceries to its lily-white customers. And you'd think, due to his occupation, he'd be quite personable. Yet other than the sadistic storekeeper and his mother, barely anyone paid him any attention. By the time Leo was 17 he weighed over 370 pounds. Yet it was not his weight that had to do with how he was perceived, but the sneer he wore upon his tremendous face. His mother Thelma, an overworked creature, widowed due to the fact her husband refused to back off the table, would've given Leo the world had it been hers to dispense with. She worked as a domestic housekeeper for the storekeeper's daughter.

The old storekeeper himself had a fondness for Leo, which rivaled that of his own children and had looked out for him since his father died. The obese boy ruled the front porch of the store from a spacious chair, which the storekeeper built especially for him. And there he sat to establish his dominance. His favorite pastime was plucking little colored boys' heads whenever they came to the store with notes of purchase. He'd often start out wrestling playfully with the children but before he turned one loose, he'd thump the child's head with all his might. And nothing pleased him more than an agonizing scream as a result of his huge knuckles. I always knew the boy suffered extreme mood swings, which determined the extent of his madness. But anytime he got hold of my brother Frankie D. or me, he'd go completely out of his head.

I could never actually rationalize any white man in the south being jealous of a black man. Yet Leo, since the day he spotted a dazzling portrait of the car in a magazine, wanted nothing more than a 1936 Chevrolet four-door Sedan. And so the day my father pulled up in his, it actually blew the boy's mind. This was six years later. So instead of getting up and rushing out to pump gas like he normally would, the boy sat on his huge rump and refused to budge. After awhile, "I know he see us," said my mother. "But if you ask me, I'd say the old dog is jealous."

Leo turned ten shades redder as he sat there looking in every direction except for where the gas pumps were situated. So my father got out and decided to approach Leo on foot. And tipping his hat he said, "How are you doing, Mr. Leo?" But Leo wouldn't speak. He just sat there, so my father decided to go on into the store. He opened the screen door and just as he was about to enter, Leo stuck his foot out and tripped him! And since a word of antagonism could've actually cost my father his life, he didn't say anything. He simply kept stumbling through the doorway.

The storekeeper, who saw the huge sneaker as Leo snatched it back, pretended he hadn't seen it. So as my father toppled through the doorway, "Watch out there," he said. "You have to be more careful." Then within the next breath or so he added, "So what can I do you out of?"

"I guess I should be more careful," said my father, "now shouldn't I?"

"You better watch out, boy," the storekeeper repeated. "So what can I do you out of?"

"I was hoping to purchase some gasoline sir," said my father. "That's if it's not too much trouble. I'll pump it myself...that's if you or Mr. Leo don't feel like it." Now I'm more than sure he'd seen my father when he arrived, yet he was as green as Leo was about the situation.

"You can't feed the shit to your mules, boy, so why do you need it?"

"I just want to purchase some gasoline, sir."

"Well, you ain't getting none here. 'Cause I ain't issuing no more credit to you nigras in the foreseen future, and probably not even until the end of the year!"

"But I've got cash money," said my father.

"Oh-oh-oh-oh-oh-oh! So you got cash money, huh?"

"At least enough to purchase some gas."

"Well, you can't feed the shit to them fucking mules of yours, can you?"

"I got an old car out here," said my father, "which Mr. Miles done help me to purchase. I'll pump it myself if I have to."

"Well," said the storekeeper reaching beneath his counter. "Since you got so much cash money, I think it's high time we settle this here account of yours." He ran his thumb across his tongue and started shuffling through his notebook. "Looks like you owe me for a five-pound sack of sugar, 50 pounds of flour, a whole entire sack of rice, and let's see... oh and what is this? Two cans of oil sausage, three containers of oatmeal – boy, you been busy at my expense, ain't 'ya?"

Finally, the old goat looked directly into my father's eyes. "You're not such a bad nigra," he said. "At least as far as nigras go. So I tell you what I'm gonna do. I'm gonna make that an even thirty-two fifty. So how about that," he said showing his palm?

"Just a minute," said Dad. "You know I can't pay you everything I owe you right now - at least not until Mr. Miles settles with me in the fall. Now you know good and well I ain't got that kind of money on me Mr. Brookings."

"Well, goddamn it. So you can drive around here in a fancy ass automobile but you can't pay your grocery bill? So what kind of shit is this," said the storekeeper looking down upon my father as if being poor was a mortal sin? But then beyond the storekeeper's nasty annoyance, a surge of negative energy went spreading throughout the store. We'd heard about the gun he had beneath his counter where he was once again reaching, an awful disturbance on his face.

'Oh, my God' my father thought, 'he's about to pull it out'. But for some reason the storekeeper had a change of heart. Instead, he looked at my father through his intricate veil of wrinkles, due mostly to years and years of living in fear and years of evil and bigotry.

44

"Since you ain't got the funds to pay your fucking bills, I don't see no advantage in doing business with you. So get the fuck out! And as far as I'm concerned, ain't no black son of a bitch who can't pay his grocery bill supposed to be riding around here in no fancy ass automobile!"

My father, on his way out the door, turned and said, "Mr. Brookings, I-mo' pray for you and ask the good Lord to forgive you and all who abuse their brethren and ..."

"Nigger, you're less than 15 minutes out the trees and you gonna tell me something about God?" He then straightened up made his final gesture toward the door. "No more credit - that's all," he said! Then over the rim of his prescription-filled bifocals, he watched my father exit the store. And it seemed he had a strong sense of potency watching him leave with the opposite attitude of which he'd arrived. And again, Leo stuck his foot out...but his timing was pathetic. So my father stepped over his bulky foot and made a final departure.

CHAPTER 9 "THE FRIDGERATOR"

Sitting on the porch in his favorite chair, the boy stuck his hand into his pocket, pulled out a dingy handkerchief and blew loudly. 'shit,' he thought. 'Not now. Any other time BUT NOT NOW! Got a icebox...iceman run twice a week! Women...they'll fuck up anything. Must be why God created 'em since that's all they ever do!' He then got up and headed up the pathway towards his mother's house. Upon his arrival, he released a huge sigh before mounting the steps, reflecting all the while on the first time my dad showed up in his car. 'The very idea,' he thought. 'Black son of a bitch pulling up in my favorite car expecting me to come out and pump his ass some gas. Well let me tell you something, you done played directly into my hands,' he thought. 'Done fucked around and fucked your own self dead in your own mother-fucking ass, that's what you done-done!'

My dad hadn't washed the car more than twice since he acquired it, which Leo considered quite trifling. He couldn't understand how my father could allow such a fine piece of machinery to morph into an old, ugly, grey, ashy looking thing. The muffler also had a hole in it, which made it sound twice as bad as it looked. But Leo knew a good wash and wax would bring it right on back up to par. So even before he acquired the funds to purchase it, he made a deal with a mechanic in Clarksdale to get a new muffler. But there was still one bridge to cross before taking control of my father's car. So he entered the cottage and slammed the door behind him as hard as he possibly could.

Thelma fell asleep listening to their only 78 RPM recording. So the boy stepped in between her and the turntable, and snatched the needle off the record. "What," she asked, startled, before Leo commenced to giving her a piece of his mind?

"Did anybody ask you for a freaking `fridgerator?"

"No, but…"

"But, my ass" he shouted! "I never asked you for no `fridgerator, did I?"

"I know," said Thelma.

"Then why in the hell did you get it, and who needs it anyhow? We already got that freaking ice box out there," he said pointing towards the kitchen.

"Aw, c'mon," said Thelma reaching in the boy's direction. "Come here, honey," she requested. But Leo refused to budge. "Please," she begged the boy, "give me a chance to explain," but he whacked her off again.

"I got the chance of a lifetime and you're trying to screw it up."

"I wouldn't do that," said his mother.

"Then why buy a `fridgerator at this time? Can't you see my back's against the wall?"

"I did it for you!"

"You ain't done shit for me," shouted Leo! "I didn't ask for no 'frigerator, let alone half the other shit you come up with around here."

"You know what the doctor said about your heart," his mother reminded him. "So why don't you sit down and relax."

And since his first law of nature was self-preservation, Leo slammed his huge rump down on the couch, buried his face in the palm of his hands then he started talking to himself.

"Got a chance of a lifetime and my own mother would rather see me rot in hell," he said while mumbling to himself.

"We is po'," said his mother, "which is a fact you have to learn to live with. And the sooner you learn, Leo, the better off you're gonna be. We all have to learn at one point or another to accept the hand we were dealt."

"Fuck that," said Leo! "About the only thing you can do for me now is to retrieve that freaking deposit."

"But I done begged until I'm blue in the face and they won't give me my money back."

"Then what you gonna do, Mama," asked the boy? "You've got to do something. 'Cause I got to have my car, Mama."

"I don't see that there's anything I can do," said his mother. "They got my money and that situation is dead, Leo. And I mean D-E-D, dead!"

48

"Then what you gonna do," asked the boy? "I'm supposed to pick up my car first thing Saturday morning!"

"Well, I don't see that there's anything I can do."

"Then ask Lilly Ruth for it, then. The bitch own half the county and I know she's got it. So why don't you ask her?"

"But I've asked her for too many advances, Leo, and most of 'em on your behalf!"

"So," said Leo. "You've been washing that bitch's dirty drawers for years on end. So it's high time she either pay-up or shut the fuck up."

"But!"

"But, my ass, this is an emergency."

Within a flash, however, Leo switched plans. He sprang up from the couch and started pacing the floor, talking to himself. "I'm-a get that car. I want that car, Mama. I'm-a get that car one way or another. Even if I have to go out and do some wrong, I'm-a get that car."

Knowing all along his mother couldn't bear the thought of him going out and robbing somebody and maybe even getting himself killed in the process, he continued to talk to himself. Almost immediately, though, Thelma broke down.

"Alright, alright," she said. "Don't try that shit on me, Leo. Now I can't make no promises except that I'll try.

I'll ask Miss Lilly Ruth but that's about the best I can do. Beyond that, your guess is just as good as mine.

"Make the bitch pay," insisted the boy. "Make the bitch fucking pay!"

"There's no guarantee," said his mother, "except that I'll try. But you've got to promise me something, too, now - just in case this don't work. You have to promise not to go out and do something stupid. Now you owe me that much, so come on and promise."

"Alright, alright," said the boy reluctantly. "So, I promise, o.k."
"Well, alright then," said his mother. "Either we can do this or we can't. And if we do, we're gonna' do it right, o.k. There's more cars where that one come from anyway, ain't it?"

Leo's demeanor took on a subtle change so he allowed the atmosphere in the room to replenish itself. He then got up and replaced the needle on the turntable. Thelma almost immediately livened up and went a-prancing through the little hallway towards the dining room, humming the Eddie Fisher song as she went along. The fact of knowing he hadn't lost his touch, Leo stuck his chest out while saying to him self, 'She just needed a little nudging that's all.'

Then Thelma suddenly needed some time alone, so she needed to get Leo out of the house. Previous bouts like this with her late husband had always left her aroused. So she stuck her fingers into her purse and pulled the

50

little pocketbook out searching for change. Other men had approached her but she remained loyal to the boy's father. So presently, she needed to attend to her own needs.

"So why," she asked, "don't you go down to the store and get us a couple of beers? It's a hot day and your mother could use a cold beer. I suppose you could use one, too."

"If I can get some bologna sausage," said Leo, "'cause I'm hungry."

So after pulling out an extra quarter, Thelma said, "Make sure you ask Stan Brookings what time Miss Lily Ruth is coming back. I wanna see about this loan of yours."

Leo stuck his hand into the cookie jar and headed out the doorway, then down the slope towards the general store. His mother stood behind the screen door watching until the obese boy disappeared beyond the slope.

52

CHAPTER 10 "YOU PLAY, YOU PAY"

On the way back from an errand one day, Leo walked up on Mr. Brookings as he was pumping gas into my father's car. And, as usual, my father and Mr. Brookings had made up. And again, he was extending my father credit.

So he motioned his head towards the store indicating my father was still inside. Leo meanwhile, pulled out a handkerchief and rubbed it on the front fender. He spat on it and rubbed it again. "Within a week's time," he bragged, "this baby's gonna be mine, all mine."

"And how did you get him to sell it," asked the storekeeper?

"I caught him messing around with that 'lil 'ole coon gal up there on Joe Adams' plantation."

"You WHAT," asked the storekeeper? "Boy, you wouldn't lie to me would you?"

"Oh, no," said Leo! "I spotted it up there several times."

"And what have you been doing hanging around up there," asked the storekeeper? "Is you been chasing that little ole' coon gal yourself?"

Leo didn't answer...yet, 'Lord,' he thought, 'how I'd love to get a taste of that 'lil 'ole foxy coon's tail!' But he would never divulge such a thing to the storekeeper, let alone anyone else.

"So how," asked the storekeeper once again, "did you get him to sell it?"

"Well," said Leo, "I saw his wife and one of them coon boys up there at the post office the other day. And did what any self-respecting white man might've done."

"And just what was that," asked the storekeeper?

"Stuck a note right under there," said Leo, "right under that windshield wiper."

"O.K." said the storekeeper, "So is that it?"

"What else," asked Leo? "Once she gets that note, the shit's gonna hit the fan! And before you know it, this baby's gonna be mine, all mine!"

"Well, I hope you don't mind but what was in that note," asked the storekeeper while checking to see if my father was coming out?

"That's my business," said Leo. "You already know too much."

"Come on," the storekeeper begged? "Don't stop now, boy! Is you gonna finish this lie or not?"

My father, whom they obviously thought was not paying attention, was looking directly at them through the store's window. He'd suspected the boy of foul play but never thought he'd stoop so very low. He knew Leo was jealous and that he wanted his car, but didn't imagine he'd go to this extreme. So, he exited the store with two sacks beneath his arms - one containing chicken feed

54

while the other contained flour. He threw them both into the back seat then told the storekeeper what he'd taken. And the storekeeper told him how much gas he'd charged him for.

He tried to avoid looking at Leo by pretending he didn't exist, so he got into his car. But just before he took off, "Alright," Leo hollered! "I'll be coming down there to get my car up pretty soon, boy. So you take damn good care of her, you hear?"

"Yassir," said my father who stuck his foot into the tank and stripped the second gear as he sped off.

Yet, he spotted the storekeeper and Leo in his rearview mirror, just a-kicking up a storm due mostly to the obese boy's impending victory.

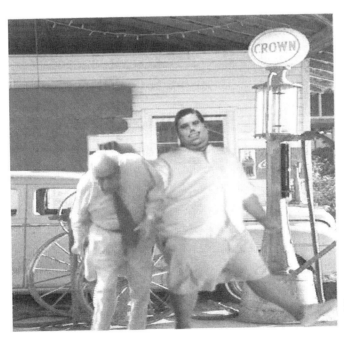

CHAPTER 11 "A MOOD FOR SOLITUDE"

Nothing I liked more than a solitary stroll along the bayou during the early morning hours. But my brother Frankie D. had formed an attachment towards me, which I rarely could escape. So I devised a plan that morning I was going to trick him. So I went into my parent's dresser drawer and I got a yellow notepad and the only crayons we had. Frankie D. followed me, all the while threatening to tell my daddy if I didn't give him one. I let him follow me. I went on back into the front room, I got down on the floor, took the crayons and I started drawing. He was still threatening to tell my dad if I didn't give him one.

So after awhile I said, "I've got to go to the outhouse." So I jumped up and ran towards the door but made the dreadful mistake of looking over my shoulder, which gave me away. Frankie D. was hip to me now. He jumped up and before I got across the road, he was right up on my back.

"Wait a minute, Frankie D.," I said, "Hold it. I just want to be alone, o.k. So please just go on back, o.k." But he just stood there puffing harder than usual, his arms across his chest. So I took him and tried to spin him around towards the shack but he spun all the way back until he was facing me again.

So I actually wanted to hit him - knock the pure-D-shit out of him - but I knew better. For no one wanted the wrath of my father to come down upon us that morning.

He and my mother had been at each other's throats for at least a week. So she was in her room, wishing she could scratch his eyes out for his indiscretions. She was also angry with herself for wanting to forgive him. Plus the fact that Leo, of all people, was about to take possession of his car, which she actually did not appreciate. But she had no choice since our entire family was at stake.

She looked out and saw my brother and I. I'm trying to avoid him going down to the stream and he's trying to make sure that he does. I was tousling with him, and so we slipped and fell. Down the bank of the bayou we went. Then we stumbled and got up, and here we go again. We kept doing that for a while and I guess it was quite amusing to my mother. I finally gave up after realizing my brother was not going away. So I threw up both hands and we rushed down to the stream together.

The dew drops on the bushes, the smell of the fern at the bank of the bayou, big frogs sitting on lily pads, and every time Frankie D. and I came close to one, it jumped off and splashed its yellow belly against the water. There were birds with pretty plumes flying around eating insects and a woodpecker high up in a tree pecking a nest for its young. All of these things were going on when we reached the bayou. I saw a cottonmouth moccasin snake swimming through the water with its head above the stream. And in the bushes, right in the sunlight, was a baby turtle, just lying there soaking up the morning sun. So I held my hands out.

"Ooh, Frankie D.," I said, "look a-there!"

Frankie D. looked at the turtle and immediately raised his foot and squashed it into a million pieces.

"What," I asked, "did you do that for?"

"Because it was ugly," said Frankie D!

"You're ugly and ain't nobody done that to you! So why did you do that to that little turtle?" He just stood there looking at me with a frustrated gaze in his eyes, as if he was trying to assess my emotions.
Realizing I wasn't going to draw any pleasure out of this outing, I decided to give it up and the two of us headed on back to the shack.

CHAPTER 12 "BACK AT THE SHACK"

We got back to the shack and Leo was already there, scrutinizing my father's car. He found little nicks and cracks here and there, but nothing out of the ordinary. Yet he was using these to manipulate my father who seemed to be going for it. "I'm sorry, Mr. Leo, but a bargain is a bargain. A bargain is a bargain, sir." But Leo paid him no attention. He just kept on scrutinizing the car and eventually asked, "Where is that fancy antenna that came with it?"

My father finally produced the thing and while he was wiping the dust from it, Leo whispered something in his ear. And whatever that was it must've had something to do with Estelle Lyle because my father suddenly shook as if struck by lightening.

"O-O-O-O.K., Mr. Leo - fifty dollars off, but that's about it, sir. Fifty dollars - that's about all I can stand."

"Good boy," said Mr. Leo. "I do have to gas this baby up, you know. And I'm gonna gas her ass up tonight!"

My father eventually gave him the keys. And once he got into the car, it appeared lopsided as he took off, a cloud of dust in its wake. We all stood by the roadside and watched him drive away in my father's car.

CHAPTER 13 "THE RUSTY DOUBLE BARREL"

Now Frankie D. and me were sitting on the steps just below my brothers Grady and James Lee, and our cousin Tyrone. It was a pitch-black night and up the gravel road came footsteps, which came closer and closer until finally they were up on the shack. We spoke to the invisible figure but it refused to speak. This was quite unusual in the rural south. So we spoke again yet it was to no avail. Then along with its footsteps, the misty shadow faded into the darkness.

My brother James Lee jumped up and ran inside to tell my father, who came a dashing through the doorway asking, "What's this I hear about footsteps?"

"It must be one of them convicts who escaped Parchman's Farm," said Grady.

"Well, whoever it was must've had something to hide," said my father. "If he wouldn't speak, he was definitely hiding something." Then suddenly our cousin, who lived a lonely existence and who also lived down the road, was afraid to go home.

"He was headed straight for our house," said Tyrone, "and I'm scared to go home. So can I spend the night here?"

"Boy," said my father, "I've got eight children of my own and I ain't got enough room for them. So no, I'm sorry but you can't spend the night here tonight."

"But I'll sleep in the barn, I'll sleep on the porch -
60

anywhere, Uncle Edmond. I'll sleep on the back porch. Just don't make me go out there on my own!"

"Boy," said my father. "The best thing I can do is to walk you home. Now that's about the best I can do." And though he wouldn't have said it to anyone less related, my father never did like overnight company.

So he went back inside and came out with his shotgun broke down beneath his right arm. "C'mon," he said. "I've got to come back and get some rest." So he and Tyrone stepped off into the darkness. Less than 45 minutes later, my father returned, the shotgun still beneath his arm. He took the thing into his room sat it in a corner, and went to sleep.

CHAPTER 14 "INEZ'S BIRTHDAY"

The next day was Saturday, the 17th birthday of my sister Inez who'd planned a swimming party down on the bayou where it turned and headed north. It was in that particular spot the bayou virtually became a treeless pool. My sister Inez, her cousins Howard and Beatrice, my cousin Tyrone, my brother Grady, my brother James Lee, my brother McClain, Inez's boyfriend Bill Williams and a host of other teenagers, all ran the last 50 or 60 yards down to the stream.

Some played at the edge while others waded into the shallows. And trying to impress Ella Mae Jones, my brother McClain swam far beyond the rest. A wonderful feat except he saw a snake swimming across his path after which he panicked. The boy completely lost control of his arms and legs, and was just about to go under when my sister's boyfriend Bill swam out to save him.

So when the party was over, on the way home, everyone was singing "She'll Be Coming 'Round The Mountain" except for Bill, who kept taunting McClain and accusing him of having a weak stroke. "You can't swim worth a shit," he told my brother as he taunted him all the way home. And once there, he told my mother how he'd saved her favorite son from drowning. They all then filed into Inez's room. And even though it was a music-less affair, they were having a lot of fun.

My father was under the influence of his sharecropping

partner Mr. Miles, who gave him the Bible and told him he was destined to become a preacher. He'd also convinced him that all African-based music - and especially the Blues - was the devil's music. He therefore would not allow us to listen to secular music. We could listen to Spiritual music, Gospel music and as strange as it seems, Country and Western! He also refused to participate in the activities since he thought Inez would compromise him in front of her peers. And since he was so determined to leave, I suspect he intended to visit with Estelle, which was a silly idea and was an act of vindication. Yet, my father went along with it anyway.

CHAPTER 15 "FOUR BITS WORTH OF CHEESE"

A girl who came by the shack on the way to the store said hello to my mother. My mother said hello and asked her where was she headed? "I'm on my way to the store," she said. "Can I get you something while I'm up there?"

"You sure can," said Mom. "I don't know what's wrong with me, child. Must be pregnant again 'cause I keep on craving cheese. Think you can bring me four bits worth?"

"I most certainly can," said the girl. "Anything else while I'm up there?"

"No honey, just some cheese." So she went into the shack, got a fifty-cent piece and sent the girl on her way.

Frankie D. and I were sitting there on the porch at my mother's feet. But as strange as it seemed, Bill was still bragging about how he saved my brother's life. And strangely enough, the children were still cackling like a bunch of noisy hens. So I got up and went inside to see what was going on. Once I entered, I ran into McClain coming through the hallway headed for my parent's bedroom to get my dad's shotgun. On the way out he ran into Jessie Mae who tried to stop him but she was eight years younger so he barely paid her any attention.

"What's wrong with you," the girl asked? "That thing could be loaded!" McClain tried to open the thing but it wouldn't budge. So he went and stood in the doorway. Bill, meanwhile, was leaning against the wall talking shit.

"I told you before we left you couldn't swim. But Na-a-h, n-a-a-h, you were just too hard headed and you wouldn't listen." The children all cracked up again. So McClain took the shotgun and aimed it at Bill's head.

"Boy, you'd rather shoot yourself before you shoot me," Bill said. "Shoot me and won't nobody be around to save your ass the next time."

And again the children burst out laughing. They were basically laughing at my brother for resorting to such an extreme.

Yet, McClain pulled the trigger but nothing happened.

"Now, you see what I mean," said the boy, "when I said you'd rather shoot yourself before you shoot me?"

So my brother messed around and pulled the second trigger. And man, oh, man, that boom reverberated! It reverberated throughout the countryside! And it seemed like the loudest thing I'd ever heard!

Bill's head splattered and went flying off his shoulders. McClain's mouth flew open but nothing escaped it!

"Lord," he eventually said! "What on earth have I done?" Inez and my cousin Beatrice scrambled to get beneath the bed. The rest of the children had no idea of what was going on! They simply sat there with their eyes and mouths wide open, none of them knowing what to do or what to say.

My mother didn't know what was going on either. Yet she knew something was mighty wrong. So she came a-rushing inside, screaming to the top of her lungs, only to see my brother standing there with the smoking gun and Bill slumped over in his chair with blood gushing from an artery slightly above his shoulder blade.

Then suddenly the children got up and went a scrambling towards the doorway. Some stopped and took a final look at the bloody corpse. Others simply covered their eyes in order not to see what was actually there. They eventually all gathered in the front yard and huddled up against one another. All except McClain who was still standing in Inez's doorway begging Bill to forgive him for killing him.

James Lee came back inside to say, "You'd better get out of here, McClain. Bill's brothers will be here any minute and they'll kill you for sure!"

"But where would I go," asked McClain?

"I don't know, but you better get the hell outta here," said my brother James Lee!

Mom came back inside, too. "Honey," she said, "you've got to get out of here! And I mean right away."

But McClain was in a stupor, so he couldn't do nothing but stand there.

Mom had always been proud of the fact that she could hold her emotions intact but from now and ever more

66

she'd never do such a thing again. Only a few words escaped her lips but they were the most powerful words she'd ever uttered.

"Come out of your stupor," she shouted, "and get the hell out of here!"

My brother broke out of his spell, dashed out the doorway then jumped on a mule Grady had saddled up for him. Grady slapped the mule on his rump and it took off like a bat out of hell!

CHAPTER 16   "FROM THE GRAVEYARD TO THE CORN PATCH"

In preparation for an orderly stroll to Grandma's house, Mom gathered the children and calmed us as best she could then instructed the older ones to keep an eye out for the younger children. Before we left, however, Bill's brother Clyde showed up on a restless mule. He was older than Bill but they'd enjoyed a close relationship.

So, angry to the core, he asked, "Which way did the motherfucker go?!"

The sheer look in his eyes frightened us out of our wits yet no one said a word. His reputation was that of a mild mannered teen who'd always respected his elders and no one had ever seen brandish a weapon.

Yet, "Somebody tell me," he begged gripping a rifle, "which way the motherfucker went!"

Sadie Mae Outlaw tried to talk him out of his obvious intentions. But, "Hell no! I'm gonna fuck him up the moment I get a bead on him! So somebody tell me which way the motherfucker went!"

"I'm sorry," said Mother, "but I don't think you understand. This was an accident, Clyde. You know my child wouldn't do such a thing on purpose!" Then she raised her head toward the sky and said, "Please Lord, endow this child with the proper understanding, and allow my child come out of this alive!"

"He's gonna need more than the Lord when I catch up with him! 'Cause when I catch up with him, I'm gonna really fuck him up. I'm gonna fuck him up real good!

"Now, Clyde ordinarily wouldn't have shown so much disrespect, so by the sheer nature of his rhetoric, we knew he meant business. The boy eventually gave up and took off in a northerly direction, which since he came from the south, was the most logical course to take.

Again my mom pleaded, "Lord, please, Lord don't let that fool catch my child!" Then, "ride honey ride," she said, as if she thought McClain could hear. "Ride like the devil himself!" We knew McClain's mule was the swiftest in the county, yet Clyde's mule appeared as if it was, fueled by greased lightening.

A mile and a half away, a piece of metal went a clanging across the road which prompted my brother to pray it wasn't Ole' Dan's horseshoe. But immediately the mule started limping. So he dismounted and walked the mule across the roadside ditch. The turf on the opposite side was softer so he remounted and took off across the empty landscape. There was an old abandoned gravesite in the distance. So he checked to see if he was followed and, lo and behold: Clyde, ahead of an awesome cloud of dust, gaining on him swiftly!

"Where," he thought, "did he come from? And where did he get such a swift-footed animal?"

By the time he reached the gravesite, Clyde was within firing range. He'd anticipated taking refuge in the corn patch slightly beyond there when Clyde fired his first shot. McClain leaped off his mule and ran into the graveyard. Clyde's second shot missed terribly so he jumped a weather beaten tombstone and headed for another. But Clyde hit the one he chose to hide behind. So when Clyde stopped to reload, McClain jumped up and ran into the corn patch. No sooner than he reloaded, Clyde fired again but with flawed accuracy.

And, according to my brother, he dove into the corn patch and got up running, splitting cornrows and knocking over corn stalks. Faster and faster he ran, and deeper and deeper into the field of maze. Then, after tripping several times, he got up and he ran even faster.

So Clyde kicked his mule profusely in an effort to reach the corn patch before my brother disappeared. But by the time he got there, he was gone. And since he could only guess which way he went, Clyde waited in total silence...but heard nothing.

McClain eventually panicked and jumped up running, so Clyde tried to cut catty-corner through the corn patch but it was futile. So he headed back toward the road in hopes of going around the corn patch and catching my brother as he emerged on the opposite side. But running as fast as possible, McClain resurfaced ahead of Clyde and, as luck would have it, spotted a couple in a T-Model Ford headed for Clarksdale. He explained his dilemma to the couple who were friends of our family and who agreed to take him to our Uncle's house several miles away. McClain took refuge there until he could board a train for Memphis.

70

CHAPTER 17 "MARCH TO GRANDMA'S HOUSE"

There were 18 of us now walking up the road towards Grandma's, all of us wailing to the top of our lungs. The girl returning from the store didn't know what to make of the weeping entourage. And my mother was so enthralled until she barely recognized the girl who'd reversed course and joined the weeping crowd. She turned to the girl behind her and asked why everyone was carrying on in such an odd manner.

"McClain," the girl said, "just shot and killed Bill Williams."

"WHAT," asked the girl?! "Please say it's not so! Please say it's not!"

"He didn't mean it," said the girl. "He was playing with an old shotgun and the thing went off."

The girl, who was Inez's age, went immediately up to Inez, wrapped her arm around her waist and marched the rest of the way. Crying and generally moping around, we spent the rest of the afternoon at my Grandmother's house.

But slightly before dusk, they sent us male children back to the scene of the tragedy where I'd never experienced anything like it before, except when Bill was shot. And from the moment we arrived, I could smell human blood, which reeked throughout the atmosphere.

My father was home now, and he and my uncle Joseph and a bunch of other men were working. He and Uncle Joe were cleaning the mess up where Bill was killed while other men brought water in from the pump and poured it through the cracks and crevices. Two men outside were digging a trench to carry bloody water from beneath the house.

I eased up on one of them and I asked him, "Is this where y'all buried poor 'ole Bill?"

"Oh, No," said the man with a hearty chuckle! "We's just trying to run some of this blood from under here."

Now, thus far, there'd been the slightest margin for laughter. Yet it was this man's chuckle that helped me to make it through that and so many other restless nights. For it was the first I'd heard since Bill's hardy chuckle, which was followed by the boisterous boom of my father's old rusty double barrel shotgun.

CHAPTER 18 "NO PUNCH LINE"

It was mid-summer and our garden was actually bursting with organic energy. And among its jewels were butter lettuce, yellow and green squash, sun-ripened tomatoes, green peas and sweet potatoes, turnips and Irish potatoes, peanuts, spinach and cantaloupe, radish and snap beans, and - most importantly - good ole' red and juicy watermelons. The only items we actually needed were things my parents could not grow such as flour, black pepper, salt and sugar, store-bought chicken feed, toothbrushes and toothpaste. But, as usual, my parents had no cash. So my father had to go to the store and open up a new account, which would make a deep cut into his prospective profits. So after allowing me to help him hook the wagon up, he climbed aboard and was just about to leave.

But I suppose the look in my eyes gave him a sense of compassion. For even at the age of six, I had eight siblings but preferred the company of my father. I felt hurt whenever my father left but always rejoiced when he returned. Yet this time he had a change of heart. So after releasing a tut, and a sigh, he instructed me to climb aboard.

As I climbed upon the wagon, my heart exploded and I suppose I was grinning from ear to ear. I was beaming so brilliantly, in any case, until my dad was compelled to relinquish his ropes to me.

"You're a big boy," he said. "So let's see if you can drive

your daddy to the store."

Since I'd never anticipated anything so far-fetched, I was petrified and suddenly felt an urge to restrain myself! I therefore sat there for a while - just sat there.

But then, "Go on, boy," he said! "You can do it! I know it's a surprise but you can do it! So let's get a move on it!"

So I popped the mules on their rumps and the wagon lurched forward.

Only two things thus far I longed for. One was to join the family in the cotton patch while the other was my passionate desire to drive my father's mule team. I'd seen him countless times navigate the wagon out the yard while always wishing I could give it a try. So now that the opportunity presented itself. I was much too overwhelmed yet performed the task with more agility than either my father or I thought I could. My mom, who was wiping her hands on an apron, stood in the kitchen window just a-chuckling as I drove the mule team pass the shack.

Both mules had opposing mannerisms. Bob, the white mule, was calm and easygoing while Ole' Dan, the black mule with a white spot amid his forehead, was a rebel who fancied his freedom more than any mule should. But my father was amazed at the black mule that day, for he was pulling his share of the weight without provocation. At least he had until we reached the crossroads in front of Mr. Miles' mansion. For it was there when he let me know who was actually in charge.

74

I thought I'd been gentle while indicating I wanted to turn there, yet he preferred a more experienced navigator.

The white mule was trying to comply but since the route Ole' Dan chose was somewhat of a challenge, there was no doubt he wanted it his way. The store was less than a half a mile from the crossroads yet the route he chose was twice the distance. He therefore was using his superior intelligence to let my father know the jig was up and that it was high time he took over. I'm more than sure my father had displayed more patience than he had done with my older brothers. But the mule was purposefully inching the rear wheels into a ditch, which left him no choice. I clearly saw it in my father's eyes. He didn't want to disappoint me but only after he took over the wagon did the mule settle down.

The storekeeper, I suspect due to my father's redeemed form of transportation, treated us like royalty that day. And, in spite of the fact that due to Leo's absence he'd fallen into a state of isolation, he was still surprisingly jovial. He gave us all sorts of free samples that day, a ritual he generally reserved for his lily-white customers. But eventually he motioned his sparsely haired head toward the door and said, "I've got something to say which I don't think you'd want this picaninny's ears to hear. So why don't we send him outside."

He'd already observed me drooling over his cold cut display, so he stuck his hand into the counter and pulled out a roll of liver sausage. Then, after mounting it on a meat cutter, he ripped a sheet from a roll of pinkish color wax paper, then cut several thin slices which he handed down to me.

"So why don't you take this, boy," he said, "and get the hell on outta' here."

So I looked up at my dad who gave me a nod of approval.

Then the old man opened the cash register and, as he removed a nickel, said, "You might as well have a soda water on me, too. Now, go on!"

I was all set to go but then my father asked, "So whata you say?"

"Oh, thank you sir," I said. "Thank you very much."

"You welcome, boy. So now get the hel outta' here."

CHAPTER 19 "OVER THE HORIZON"

I attempted to work the Coca-Cola machine the moment I stepped out on the porch but the powerful scent of the liver sausage proved a lesser challenge. So I climbed into Leo's chair and devoured the first slice but then I heard a humming noise that sounded like nothing I'd heard. So searching the expanse for its source, I spotted this strange looking apparatus which was coming up the railroad tracks and which practically scared the living daylights out of me! The long, sleek looking thing came a-creeping up the railroad tracks like nobody's business on wheels like those of a boxcar. In all my days, I'd never dreamt such a thing existed. Yet there it was: a long, dark blue, 1939 Buick limousine which came a-creeping up the railroad tracks in broad daylight!

So to the storekeeper's surprise, and I'm sure my father's delight, I ran back into the store screaming, "Daddy, Daddy! There's something coming up the railroad that you just gotta see! So please, Daddy, please hurry!"

He'd already grown tired of the old man's racially charged jokes. So, "Oops," said my father, while straightening up and heading for the doorway. I was directly ahead of him, pointing towards the unusual contraption in, which were six solemn faced men, all of whom wore dark colored suits and ties. There was no steering device, just six stone-faced men who, with lethargic stares, appeared akin to the mannequins in the storefronts of Clarksdale. My father hadn't seen anything like it, either. Yet common logic told him what it was. But still the sight of those stone-faced men must've also given him an eerie sensation.

The storekeeper responded to my squeaky voice, too, which prompted him to come outside, as well. But no sooner than he spotted the thing he said, "Now them guys there, that's the big cheese there, 'n they call themselves Railroad Executives. And from what I've heard, they don't take no shit, either." Then he turned to my father and asked, "Know what I mean, boy?"

"Yassir," said my father. "Railroad 'zecutives."

I'd never seen anything like this nor heard such a word so I became quite confused. The storekeeper didn't like anyone cutting in on his jokes so he was hot under the collar. Meanwhile, I'm struggling to understand the term at the same time he's insisting on regaining my father's attention. I'm also wondering where this big hunk of cheese is he mentioned. Is it in the trunk or maybe in the hubcaps? I started drilling my father and asked him to help me with the Coke machine. But the storekeeper was seething and probably was thinking, 'I've been too nice to these black son-of-a-bitches today and I'll be damned if this one ain't gonna hear me out!'

As far as he was concerned, my father was the seat of his dilemma anyway, for had he not sold his car to Leo, he wouldn't be so God-awful lonely. Eleven years they'd shared a relationship. But since he'd acquired the car, Leo had all but abandoned both him and his grocery store.

I could tell my dad was trying to figure out how he was

78

going to explain to me why he told the old bigot he understood when he actually had no idea of what that word meant. He understood the big cheese terminology yet wasn't sure he could explain that properly.

Amid the confusion, the old man's anger reoccurred. "Goddammit," he yelled! "What's more important? What I'm trying to say here or you fetching that coon a soda water?"

"I'm sorry, sir, but this is my offspring you're talking about."

"So! If it wasn't for me he wouldn't even have no soda water," recanted the storekeeper, after which he rushed back towards the screen door. "I tell you what," he said. "You'd better get what you come for and get the hell on before I change my mind, in which case you won't get a goddamn thing!" He then went deeper and deeper into the store mumbling.

'Why,' he asked himself, 'do I waste my time with any of these no account son-of-a-bitches? Ain't a single one of 'em worth a quarter in Mexican money.'

Though he couldn't afford to reveal his rage my father felt an urge to clear his mind.

"Well, since that's the way you feel, sir, then I probably should take my business elsewhere. Frankly, sir, I don't see why anyone should have to go through all of this just to buy some groceries!"

"Watch your mouth now, boy. Watch your goddamn mouth," the storekeeper warned. "I suggest you don't forget who you're dealing with!"

"But you don't have to talk to a man like he's got a tail on him, sir. Especially in front of his child! Now, I know you know what the Good Book says, sir. It says, 'Those who...'"

"Hold it, hold it, hold it," exclaimed the storekeeper, "now just a goddamn minute, boy. Now you know I can't take that shit to the bank, don't you," he said as if he'd never been angry in the first place? "I'd rather give you my entire inventory than to go through that shit again! You certainly know how to get next to an old fart, now don't you?" Again he started mumbling. "Don't know what's wrong with nigras nowadays. Come to just a-getting all upset over a joke or two. Ain't that a bitch?"

He once again looked down at me. "Boy, stick your hand on down in that barrel and load up on some of them dried apples."

But I looked up at my father who, after a slight hesitation, said "I'm sorry, sir, but this boy done had enough junk for today. But thank you anyway." Which obviously made him feel less sure-footed.

"Stick your hand down in there, boy," he insisted, "and load up on some of them dried apples!" But to ensure I wasn't going against my father's wishes I simply wrapped both arms around my father's thigh.

"I don't mind," my father said, "doing business with you, Mr. Brookings. But only if you stop disrespecting me in front of this child."

80

"Good boy," he said as if my father's words had no significance. "So, let's get right on down to it then." And, of course, he wanted my father's business. So he stepped back behind the counter and he reached under it for his notebook. "O.K., now, so what'll it be? Five pounds of sugar, a 10 pound sack of flour, two tins of black pepper, 32 ounces of salt, three cans of oil sausage, two sacks of chicken feed and a dozen lemons, 12 toothbrushes and five tubes of toothpaste. So now is that it?"

"Yes sir. I think that just about ought to do it," said my father.

He then silently wrote down 15 cent for an eighth pound of liver sausage and five cents for a Coca-Cola. Then he slowly eased his notebook back under the counter.

But "don't you have something for me to sign," my father asked?

But after locking eyes with my dad, "That won't be necessary," he said, "since you know I actually trust you. We've had our ups and downs, but you're not such a bad nigra after all. So what's this I hear about you preaching lately? Now is that so?"

"Oh, yes sir," said my dad. "The Good Lord called me pretty near four years ago."

"Well I'll be doggone," said the storekeeper. Hell, by the time I hit the dirt, you might be eligible to preach my funeral. Hell, it won't matter then anyway, would it?

[Chuckle, chuckle, chuckle] Times are a-changing, you know." [Chuckle]

"Well," said my father, "but I don't think they're a-changing quite that fast sir. But you have a good day anyway, okay."

CHAPTER 20 "SWEET PERFUME DOES NOT MIX WITH GASOLINE"

Estelle finally became a thing of the past, and my mom and my dad were at one with each other again. Since my father hadn't seen Estelle, he'd finally conquered his overblown ego - or at least it seemed so. But Grady and he were headed home one afternoon with four barrels of water on back of the wagon. Leo came swooshing by in my dad's refurbished car, which all but frightened Daddy's mules off the road. And to his great surprise, Estelle was in the car with the boy, and the two of them were laughing up a storm! My dad, meanwhile, did his best to regain control of his mule team.

Leo showed up at our house the next day to show us all the enhancements he'd made on the car, knowing all along that each was breaking my father's heart. Yet he kept on bragging. He'd added a silver decorated lady with wings who leaned forward on the hood, a coon's tail attached to her feet, a beige steering wheel cover, accompanied by a beautiful purple and blue knob. There were fancy flaps with silver tips protecting the rear wheels which made the car look twice as good as it did when my father purchased it. But what truly got to my father was Estelle's perfume, which saturated the entire fabric of the car's interior. And I could tell, even though he tried to hide it, how my father was suffering in anguish! Yet the boy insisted on showing him everything he'd done in detail.

During their conversation, he offered my father a bet on

the fight between Max Schmeling and Joe Louis to which Daddy said he wouldn't bet on a sure thing since he'd become a Christian. The obese boy said he'd heard practically every Negro would be betting on Joe Louis, yet he hadn't ran into a single white man in his right mind who'd bet against Schmillen. So he was looking for all the Negro bets he could get his hands on.

"You just tell 'em," he said pounding him self in the chest, "Mr. Leo is taking all bets regardless of the size!"

He then got back into the car and started the engine. But he didn't leave. He just sat there with the front seat back as far as possible, his potbelly protruding and slightly touching the steering wheel. He allowed the engine to run while he talked and bragged and talked and bragged and talked. Frankie D. and I got tired of him so we went up on the porch to talk about all the things we'd love to do to him as a result of our scorn - none of which were nice - then went around to the side of the shack and played marbles until the obese boy finally tired himself of bragging and left.

CHAPTER 21 "HOW CAN YOU SING ANOTHER MAN'S BLUES?"

My dad's energy level hit rock bottom after that and all he could do was mope around the shack. Good thing, though, because it was the only time of year he could afford such a luxury. Mom felt responsible so she cooked him practically every dish she thought he'd enjoy, including his favorite deserts like sweet potato pies, peach cobblers and rich pound cakes - but all of this might as well been sawdust.

Both Estelle and Leo played over and over in the theater of my father's mind, just a-laughing and making silly jokes about him. He tried to block them out but they'd be replaced by X-rated versions. One version displayed Porky Pig as he approached Estelle's place. And after walking right past my dad, he grabbed Estelle and clamped his fish-like lips onto one of her nipples. He then slid his malicious tongue all the way up her seductive neck and then rammed it down into her throat. And since Porky was white and my dad wasn't, there was nothing he could do except toss and turn.

Eventually he came down with flu-like symptoms. Yet my mother, who was determined to take care of him, was vigilant. She knew whatever was wrong with him had to do with Leo and his car yet couldn't understand why he'd trip out over such a silly thing. But in order to cheer him up, she suggested he'd own a better car some day. "Yes, you will," she said. "Just wait and see...you just wait and see..."

CHAPTER 22   "WHY LET YOUR GREED OUTDO YOUR NEED"

As a victim of circumstance, my father developed a habit of sunup 'til sundown drudgery. He forced us to work 40 acres of old man Miles' fertile land practically free of charge. Our entire family lived and breathed a daily dose of humility. And during our entire careers, merely came close to breaking even, but only twice. My dad and Mr. Miles had entered into a 50/50 agreement. Where as: they were supposed to split the profits straight down the middle. So after paying the shyster $12.50 per acre, we were supposed to earn our share by cultivating, planting, chopping and picking cotton. So at the end of the season, Mr. Miles and my dad would sit down to discuss their differences, hence a process called "settlement time."

There was a time, though long forgotten, when my parents kept records - until they grew tired of wasting pencils and paper. Since, added to his propensity to manipulate the price of cotton, Mr. Miles had a habit of ignoring my parents' count. His motto, which said, "A nigger is at his **B**est when **B**ent until **B**roken," and which he referred to as, "The Triple B System." He often bragged of the fact that he only worked on The Triple B System, yet no one knew exactly what that meant. Some field hands questioned it among themselves, but in a joking manner and without the collective guts to confront the old shyster. My dad gathered the courage once, but the ole' rotten toothed scoundrel simply hit him up with one of his corny ass jokes.

Practically all of his sharecroppers barely made it through the winter. And in order to do so, one would have to borrow on the next year's crop, which threw them deeper and deeper into his debt.

His Greek-style mansion, in contrast to their miserable existence, was a huge white structure trimmed in green with six huge columns supporting the roof of the front porch with a 60-pound chandelier, surrounded by a stairwell, that spiraled its way up to the second floor. The house was built at the turn of the century and had a den, which could accommodate a string quartet and several dozen guests. The dining room was bigger than my parents' bedroom and the kitchen extended into a maids quarters. His bedroom, library, private study and walk-in closet were also situated on the ground level.

[tense shift]

Betty Jo, his wife who was 20-some-odd years his junior, hated his guts, chewing habit and the male species in general. She'd long since moved into her quarters on the second floor where she hired and fired maids until she came across Janice LaRue, a creamy mulatto who was more than willing to satisfy Betty Jo's freakish desires. And, of course, none of this sat well with the old man who'd embellished his habit of kicking Negroes around since she'd abandoned his bedroom. All except for Henrietta McGee whose cooking, he was convinced, he couldn't live without.

Henrietta was the only one in the household who'd won the old man's total respect. And this she did one Saturday morning during a violent confrontation. Being

87

that it was the weekend and no one was around, she taught the old goat a valuable lesson. After he slammed a tray of hot oatmeal and coffee up against her face during a temper tantrum, busting both Henrietta's lips, she beat the holy shit out of Mr. Miles and left him with two less tobacco-stained teeth! By the time he came to, she'd split and hid out with relatives until she could board a train for St. Louis. Upon her arrival there, she landed a job in a soul food restaurant. Less than a year later, however, she knocked on his door and asked for her job back and she's been there ever since.

He also had this 60 year-old Negro houseboy who'd eat his refuse upon request, and who'd assisted him in becoming one of the most spoiled, rude and uncouth individuals in God's creation - a rascally scoundrel who'd long since lost interest in cleaning up after himself and who chewed two packs of Bloodhound Tobacco daily which he'd rarely spat beyond his personal effects. His twenty some-odd suits, as were his sport jackets, were inundated with urine and chewing tobacco stains. And it's altogether possible, without a lucrative inheritance, he wouldn't have been worthy of the least respect, whatsoever.

And though there may have been a time when he was productive, he'd been reduced in his dotage to a mere nuisance who drove around wreaking havoc on Negro field hands. His son, Edward Jr., lived several miles away and oversaw his personal affairs. His ambition was to follow in his father's footsteps, which was a prospect none of his field hands looked forward to. For it was rumored the son was twice as cruel as his father

88

was before him.

CHAPTER 23 "ROLLING IN THE CORN PATCH"

He'd often drive his Ford Coupe out of his tree-lined driveway then head north or south depending on which field hands he intended to antagonize. And this he'd already made up his mind to until he spotted Leo passing in my father's car, which upset him to no end. So he followed the obese boy to his assumed destination. But heading towards Tut Willey, Leo drove right on past our place. Meanwhile, old man Miles made a swift turn into our yard, knocking down cornstalks, as he cascaded into my father's pigpen, causing hogs to go scattering into all directions, only to realize he was stuck among goo-gobs of filthy shit!

My dad and my two older brothers were working in the corn patch. So my dad, he rushed out to see what was going on. Only to discover the old man sitting in the middle of the pig pen with an unconcerned expression as he rocked back and forth right along with his car. Steam shot up from the radiator and smoke from the manifold was building up beneath the car. Yet he simply sat there just a-rocking back and forth. He eventually noticed my dad and eased up off the gas.

"Well," he asked? "What the fuck are you waiting for? Get me outta here!"

My father yelled for the two boys to come and help him push the car out of the mess. My brothers came out and went to the front of the car to push the car backwards. But my father, who looked around the side, realized it was futile. The old man had panicked and put the car into first gear. My dad went to the driver's side yelling. "Mr. Miles," he screamed! "You're grinding in the wrong direction!" Finally, Mr. Miles noticed my dad and eased up off the gas. My brother James Lee suddenly busted out laughing. But my father looked at him with a stern expression, so he and my brother Grady ran back into the corn patch where they rolled in the dirt to the point of exhaustion.

My father, meanwhile, said, "Don't worry, Mr. Miles. We're gonna get you outta here one way or another. I'm gonna go fetch my mule team and everything's gonna be just fine, you just wait and see."

He then walked off to a wall of cuss words. My brothers eventually stopped laughing and went in search of the missing animals. They caught a young male and tied its feet, then left it at the edge of the corn patch.

My mother, meanwhile, was busy trying to plug up our mouths. For this was the first time we'd had the old shyster at a disadvantage, of which he'd always had over us. So we were having a natural ball! My father finally returned with his mule team, but the old man, who was hot under the collar, demanded him to hurry up and get him out of there. But, for once in his life, my father ignored the shyster. He took his dear ole' time, he dawned himself with his hip boots, then he hooked the mule team up and the affair was over.

CHAPTER 24 "THE ALTERCATION"

After an hour of onerous effort they'd captured all the pigs except a single female. So burnt out and smelling like shit, my dad marched his mules past the old man's car.

But, "Hold it," said Mr. Miles!

Then, after spending a nominal amount of time situating a beige rubber tipped cane on the ground, he crawled out and walked the length of his car on wobbly legs.

"We gotta talk," he said.

"Yes sir, Mr. Miles...but my mules, sir."

"Fuck that! So what happened to the car I bought you?"

"You helped me to get it, sir, but I paid for it, remember?"

"But I gave you the down payment for it, didn't I?"

"Yes sir," said dad. "But you took that out of last year's settlement, sir, and more beside."

"I still gave it to you, didn't I?"

"Yes sir, but I've been paying you back."

"So where's the car now?"

"I'm sorry, sir, but I had to sell it."

"YOU WHAT? Did I give you permission to sell that

92

car?"

"No sir, but due to circumstances beyond my control!"

"Well, who in the hell did you sell it to?"

"Mr. Leo"

"What? You sold my car to Leo Clark?"

"I'm sorry but I had to."

"I didn't give you permission to sell that car, did I?"

"No sir."

"Well, what'd he give you for it?"

"Well, with due respect," said Dad, "since I paid for it, I don't quite think that's none of your business."

"Where in the hell do you get off telling me what's my business? Every goddamn thing - and I mean every goddamn, cock-sucking thing around here - is my business. And I mean every cock-sucking thing!"

"I know sir," said Dad, "but-"

"Ain't no ifs, ands or buts about it," said Mr. Miles! "I said everything, and that includes every penny you lay your black ass hands on, you understand? So where is my share of the profits?"

"Since I paid for it, sir, with my own money and more beside, I figured whatever I got was mine to keep."

"And what do you mean, boy, 'more besides?' Is you

suggesting I done cheated you out of something? Nigger is you trying to make some sort of a smart ass accusation or what?"

His face now was redder than a beet and his aging limbs were shaking like an animated sifter.

"Who gave you the authority to think anyhow," said Mr. Miles, pointing his cane at my father. "Listen up you black son-of-a-bitch! We're in a profit sharing business here, which means fifty percent of every dime you lay your black ass hands on is mine!"

He then raised his cane as if he was about to strike my father over the head. I'd already snuck up behind them and stood witness to the crux of their conversation. So I picked up a stick and ran to within feet of them both. Approaching them from behind, I practically frightened the wits out of both he and my dad.

"I dare you," I shouted! "I double dog dare you! Don't you hit my daddy with that thing!"

And being that he wasn't quite sure of how to react, the old man looked down at me in stark surprise. I remember I had my jaws all puffed out as if it made me appear bigger than I actually was.

And since his temperament had succumbed to astonishment, he turned to my dad and asked, "WHAT?" Then he turned back to me, "Boy, is you done lost your mind?" Then again back at my father. "Where did you get this silly ass some-bitch from?"

After finally collecting his wits, my dad said, "Boy, if you

94

don't get your silly tail back in that house, I'll take my belt off and wear your tail out with it!"

With naked fear overtaking him, he turned again to face the old man who'd suddenly burst into uncontrollable laughter! So suddenly my father was both bewildered and in total shock! Mr. Miles, meanwhile, was salivating all over the place, and was laughing in a manner no one even imagined he could. So cautiously, as if he'd fallen under the old man's spell, my father followed suit. And before you knew it, they were both holding their stomachs. Mr. Miles was spewing tobacco juice in practically every direction while my father became so unglued until he actually buckled to his knees.

My mother, who'd apparently watched it from afar, came a running out to snatch me up by the shoulders and shook me violently while dragging me back towards the shack. Then she admonished me to never do such a thing again. So both shaken and confused, I burst out crying. Yet, any other time, she would've beat me to a pulp and my father would have done the same thing later. But since I had single handedly altered a grave contingency, I guess she decided – for at least just this once- to let me slide.

CHAPTER 25 "ODE TO MR. MILES

My mother explained how a Negro was never supposed to strike a white person – NEVER - which she rationalized by saying Mr. Miles had a natural inclination to argue.

"He knows he's wrong," she said. "And so do we. But he seem to get such a kick out of it."

That made it sound like their sole obligation was to justify his pathetic ailment, as if it was their moral obligation to comply with his twisted outlook. But from my point of view, it was at the expense of them becoming neurotics, too. So now I'm wondering why my father, whom, in my mind, was one of the greatest people on the planet, should have to put up with this old shyster's convoluted bullshit, when all he did was ride around daily promoting misery? And since my parents were twice as wise as I, why would they continuously tolerate such a nerve-racking situation?

I'd occasionally watched the ole' charlatan grab my father by the collar and shake him till he was a nervous wreck. And what did my father do? He came into the shack, knelt down on his knees and prayed for the Lord to forgive poor ole' Mr. Miles, for he knows not what he do. And that, of course, was the biggest hunk of shit I'd ever heard. The hell if he didn't know! The old bastard knew exactly what he was doing.

But why would such a religious man as my father, who claimed to know all about right and wrong, be so willing to validate his wicked behavior? Even at six years-old, these were contradictions which I found difficult to process. Yet it did little to stop me from being disappointed for the part my father played in such an awkward situation.

CHAPTER 26 "JOE LOUIS AND MAX SCHMELING"

On the night of the fight, we gathered around the radio listening to the news by Gabriel Heater who mentioned the fight before leaving the air. Everyone in the shack was stimulated by the prospect of a Louis victory. So the excitement among us escalated and at 8PM, the bell rang. Then after a brief introduction, the fight was on. And less than a minute into the ordeal, my mother said, "Kill 'em Joe!"

The voice on the radio was becoming more and more intense. "Louis," it said, "hooks a left to Max's head quickly, then shoots over a hard right to the head. Louis shoots a left to the jaw, a right to his head. Max shoots a hard right to Louis's head. Louis, with the old one-two - first a left and then a right - he's landed more blows in this round than in five rounds of their other fight."

Then, unexpectedly, Edna Rea - one the youngest siblings - said, "Kill him, Joe! Kill that sucker!"

We all turned and looked at the girl in stark surprise. Then, after a brief outburst, my mother applied a finger to her lips.

Leo, who'd bet every cent, was on top of the world! And while anticipating his winnings, held a beer in one hand and a bologna sandwich in the other as he and Thelma leaned forward on the couch. The entire pride of the south, as far as he was concerned, was riding on his speculations. And had Hitler ran for office that day, he and a host of southerners may have voted for the shyster. So he was hyped up and wouldn't allow his mother to speak during the fight. And the few times she tried, he raised a rib-like hand to muffle her mouth.

"Alright," he shouted. "C'mon now, Max. Atta boy, Max! Turn him around now! Turn him around, Max! Turn the black son-of-a-bitch around! Yeah, Maxie, that's it! That's it!" But then, "Oh, no, get outta there! Get outta there! Come on, Max and get outta there! Now push him back. Push him back, Max! Come on, Max! Push the-" But then Louis hit Schmeling with something a comatose horse could've felt, to which Leo immediately started choking on his sandwich.

Up from the couch sprang Thelma. "Jesus," she shouted! "What on earth are you doing? What are you doing, Leo? What the- don't go getting all upset over this silly 'ole fight. It's just a fight, honey! Can you hear me? Leo? Lord," she screamed! "Help me, Jesus! Somebody please!"

Clutching his chest and gasping for air, Leo tried to speak but nothing escaped the boy's lips. Thelma, who'd succumbed to hysteria, tried to break his fall but since he was so hefty, she found it much too difficult. And judging from the way his head hit the floor she knew it was something he wouldn't be getting up and walking away from. It was obviously a heart attack or a massive stroke.

So "Why," she asked, as if thought Leo could comprehend? "Why did you allow yourself to get all involved?" And though she realized it was an emergency, she was reluctant to leave him alone. 'What," she thought, 'if he die?' 'I'll never see him alive again!' The very idea sent chills up her spine. And 'Oh, my God,' asked Thelma. 'What am I supposed to do?'

Leo, with his eyes rolled up in back of his head, tried to speak but could only manage a faint whisper. "Go get Doc Rainey," he said lifting his sleepy arm. "Go get Doc Rainey ..." Thelma headed for the door but, thinking, 'should I leave,' she turned and extended her arms in the boy's direction. But Leo repeated, "Mama, please go, go get Doc. Rainey ..."

So out the door she ran. Down the slope towards Doc Rainey's, which was only slightly beyond there yet it seemed like a thousand miles. Finally, when she reached his doorstep, he, too, was cussing Joe Louis from here to hell and back, and, as usual, was in an ossified stupor. "I'll be damned," he complained, "if you don't pick the dandiest times, Thelma."

But, "Doc, its Leo," exclaimed Thelma! "He's choking on a bologna sandwich and I think he's having a heart attack!" Taken totally by surprise, Doc Rainey grabbed his stethoscope, rushed outside then took his bag from the trunk of his automobile.

"Hop on in," he said. "I'll drive us back up the hill."

They arrived within seconds and immediately were up on the porch. Thelma gritted her teeth before reentering the cabin. Doc Rainey, who went in ahead of her, simply knelt down and shook his head. Again she fell to her knees and tried to lift the boy up but settled for holding

100

his head in her lap. She sat there for the longest rocking his head back and forth. Finally, she struggled to her feet and threw herself into the doctor's arms. Then buried her face against his shoulder. "I knew I shouldn't have left him," she cried. "Lord knows I didn't want him to die like this, all alone by himself. That was the last thing I wanted."

"Aw, c'mon," said the doctor. "Don't be so hard on yourself. You did exactly what you were supposed to do."

Still she insisted, "I didn't want him to die all alone like this."

"But," said Doc. Rainey patting her on the back, "you actually did what you were supposed to do." Then he held her off far enough to look into her eyes and to assure her that death is the ultimate friend to life. And that it was altogether possible that her son was in a better place.

Three days later, a huge grave was dug. And as Leo's coffin was drawn towards it by six decorated horses, four of which were black and the leading two white, his veiled faced mother walked arm and arm with Doc Rainey who had alcohol oozing from his pores. Then Brookings, the sadistic storekeeper, and his daughter Lily Ruth - both benefactors of this elaborate undertaking - crept along in the funeral procession. Curious onlookers gathered on the side of the road - the blacks who did, only did so momentarily. For there was a sign at the entrance of the cemetery, which simply read: "WHITE ONLY."

102

CHAPTER 27 "THE WEIGHT OF COTTON/ THE WEIGHT OF GOLD"

While displaying a willingness to be groomed, Mother Nature exposed her diversity. She adorned herself with dense pods which displayed her bountiful abundance then flung the spectacle across the floor of the Delta - and oh, what a spectacle to behold! And suddenly, there was cotton for as far as the human eye could see.

So, with two barrels of water sloshing back and forth on the wagon, Dad and I were headed home. Ole' Dan was protesting but only enough to let me know he wasn't quite ecstatic. And since there were no turns to negotiate that day, the arrogant mule was not the dominant factor.

We had less than a half a mile to go when Dad dropped the bomb on me. "You're a big boy," he said. "And I always promised whenever I thought you were ready, I was..." but he never finished.

"You sure," I exclaimed, my heart pounding? "You really mean it? You gonna let me go to the cotton patch? You really mean it?"

"It's about time," said my daddy. "I see what you can do. But you can't be letting me down though, you understand?"

"Oh, daddy, I won't let you down," I said! "I'm gonna be the best cotton picker you ever had, you just wait and see."

"Good boy," he said. "Cause I'll be counting on you."

"Oh, my God," I shouted. "Finally, I'm gonna get a chance to pick some cotton!"

"You got that right," said my dad as he sat erect with a huge smile.

Clasping my hands, I raised my head to the sky. "Thank you, Lord. Thank you," I said, with my eyes tightly closed. "And thank you, too, Daddy."

"So what's that all about," he asked?

"For being the best dad in the whole wide world."

So, blushing and displaying a huge measure of pride, "Well, alright then," he said, "I'm taking your word for it, alright. You're gonna be my best cotton picker, right?"

"Yes sir," I repeated.

"Well as long as you don't let me down boy," he said. "Because I'm starting you out first thing Monday morning."

"Oh, Daddy, I'll never let you down! I promise."

As soon as we got home, I jumped off the wagon singing. I skipped across the yard singing,

"Nah, nah, nah-nah, nah / I'm gonna pick some cotton / Nah, nah, nah-nah, nah / I'm gonna pick some cotton"

104

My brothers Grady and James Lee, who were playing marbles in the front yard, gave me the once over. And though they looked at me as if I'd lost my mind, I skipped right on past them repeating,

"Nah, nah, nah-nah, nah"

So leaving them shaking their heads, I ran up on the porch and yanked the screen door open. Frankie D. whose heart practically hit the floor, fell in behind me with a single suspender strap dragging the floor behind him. So I stopped and with a hard face said, "You're too young to be picking cotton, so just back off. Back off, okay?"

No doubt the rude remark cut him to pieces and I'm sure he was wondering why his favorite brother suddenly turned on him. Yet bent on telling Mom, I kept singing and a-skipping towards the kitchen.

"I'm gonna pick some cotton / I'm gonna pick some cotton / Nah, nah, nah-nah, nah"

"I know, I know," said Mom. "I heard you all the way out there in the front yard. So you're going to be a good field hand, eh?"

I know my eyes were sparkling and though I believed she would've given me a hug, Frankie D. was standing there with a painful expression. So she picked him up instead and assured him that he too would be joining the family in the cotton patch one day.

"But trust me," she added. "It ain't all its cranked up to be. Now I know your daddy promised to take you to the cotton patch next week, but that don't give you no right to be mean to your brother. So you apologize to this child right away and I mean right this minute."

"But mama..." I complained.

"Do as I say, boy! And apologize to this child."

"Ok," I said dropping my head. "I'm sorry, Frankie D."

"Now that's better," said Mom. "You probably wouldn't like it out there anyway," she told my brother, which didn't seem to make him feel any better. "And your brother here," she said, "might be in for a surprise or two, himself. Meanwhile, I need you to do something for me. I need you to look out for your sister just like C. W. looked out for you. You think you can do that?"

"Yasum," said Frankie D., still pouting.

"You sure?"

"Yasum."

"Well alright then," said our mother. And though her request and words of encouragement were comforting, I could tell my brother still felt as though he was left out of the equation.

CHAPTER 28 "FORK IN THE ROAD"

As Monday morning converged upon me, I found it difficult to sleep. Within the periodic moments that I did, I dreamt of cotton - big fluffy pillows of it, which I jumped up and down and turned summersaults on. I missed two consecutive nights of rest. Then come Sunday night, even though I was totally exhausted, my father had to force me to go to bed. Yet all I did was toss and turn and listen to Frankie D. snore. In the wee hours of the morning, I finally drifted off and was in no mood to be disturbed when my father came in to wake us up. By the time I made it to the kitchen, I was much too excited to eat. My mother tried to force me to eat something but being that I was so overwhelmed, I simply could not find the time to eat.

Now Jessie Mae was usually the first one out the door but I was right up on her this time. So not being so pleased with my eagerness, she propositioned me to pick right along beside her. I couldn't help but notice the devilish look in her eyes.

So, "I'm picking along beside my daddy," I retorted to which she spewed a ghastly expression. The expression was designed to be-puzzle me. So I ran back up on the porch, "Is y'all coming out or not," I yelled?

"Listen at this boy," my father said a-busting through the doorway. "You really mean business, don't you?"

"Yes sir! But what's taking y'all so long," I said?

"They'll be out soon," said my father. "Don't you be so impatient - that cotton ain't going nowhere!"

And as soon as everyone assembled, Jessie Mae led us past the truck garden and through the corn patch then finally into a sickly patch of cotton where I stopped and asked, "Can we start here?" Which prompted my siblings to burst out laughing.

"Oh, no," said my mother looking down upon me admirably. "That's the last cotton we're going to pick - that's if we get to it at all."

"Well there ain't no ifs, ands or buts about it this time," said Dad. "With this kind of enthusiasm, we're gonna be looking for more cotton before it's over."

My mother said, ignoring his optimism, "Don't worry. There's gonna be lots of cotton where we're headed." My brothers James Lee and Grady were snickering behind my back, and I was wondering why, but still I gave them the benefit of the doubt. We continued walking until we came up on another dirt road which we turned on and walked another quarter of a mile or so. We passed a storage shed where everyone stopped. My dad stepped between these two rows, which he tested earlier to make sure the crop was ready to be picked.

He then reached in his sack and pulled out another one - a gunnysack - which he proceeded, to crown me with. He unfolded the thing then, taking his time, he positioned the string around my neck. Then after he tucked it beneath my arm, he positioned it across my

109

back then stood back and he scanned me approvingly. "Now that," he said, "if ever I saw one is a perfect fit!"

He took the two rows next to me and, once again, Jessie Mae asked if I could pick next to her. But, "No," said my mother. "Your dad and I want to keep an eye on this boy, just in case he falls behind."

"But I'm not gonna fall behind," I said, to which no one said a word.

"C'mon now," said Mom. "Pick right here between your dad and me so we can help you out in case you do fall behind. You are new at this game ain't you?"

"Yassum."

"Then go on up there and start on that pre-picked row before I lose my patience."

Then, wracking my brain, I was trying to figure out why they were making such a fuss over me. I was gonna pick rings around the lot of them as far as I was concerned.

But "I ain't gonna need no help," I repeated.

To which my father said, "Y'all leave this boy alone." So after taking a final glance, he bent over and started picking.

Moments later, I was still grinning - grinning from ear to ear. But that's when I spotted Jessie Mae who was already passing me up. That's when it dawned on me that this was not a plaything. I stuck my finger on a prickly cotton bulb, which drew a few crimson drops of

110

blood. So after screaming, "YEOWW," which my parents responded to, I approached my father with my finger raised.

"Look Daddy, it's bleeding!" I said.

But without the least bit of sympathy, "I see son," He said. "You got to pick the cotton out of them things instead of sticking them in your fingers. So now put that sack back on and let me see what you can do. I want to see how much cotton you can put in that sack!" Then he added, "I guess you can see what your mama and me been talking about now, huh?"

My parents doubled back to catch me up. So I turned to look and see what everyone else was doing. James Lee and Grady were slightly ahead of my parents who'd at least been even with them if they hadn't stopped to help me. So now I'm wondering, since I was still struggling to gain a foothold, if they had some sort of a secret or another. I barely saw anyone ten minutes later but heard my father as he headed back towards me.

"Boy," said my daddy, "you've got to do better than this, okay? So c'mon now `cause I know you can do better?"

Jessie Mae, meanwhile, had all but disappeared, which was par for the course according to what I'd heard. Yet even with the help of my parents, I hadn't caught up with Edna Rea who was actually lagging behind everybody! James Lee and Grady were completely out of sight, and my dad was becoming more and more agitated.

111

The twine strap was cutting into my shoulder so I decided to try and switch it to the opposite side, which felt quite awkward. So, "C'mon," my father said again! "You can do better than this, can't you?!"

"But," while struggling to adjust my sack, "I'm doing the best I can," I said. But then I suddenly felt disgusted once I looked back at my sack, which appeared to have a hole in it!

And again I heard my father, "I'm catching you up one more time," he said. "But after that you're on your own."

So finally, when he picked his way back to me, his sack was half full. But a single look at mine and he went off. "

Boy," he shouted! "Is that all the cotton you've got?! I thought you was gonna be a good field hand! So what are you doing out here anyway?"

I looked up at him with a frustrated gaze and I told him, "I'm doing the best I can."

"Aw NAW boy, can't you do better than that?" You can do better than that, can't you?" but there was no reply.

"Do you hear me?!"

"Yassir."

"Well then answer me!"

I'm more than sure he didn't appreciate my frustrated gaze, which was something he must've considered out of character.

112

"Anytime I'm talking," he shouted, "I expect your full attention! Do youunderstand?"

I answered but apparently not loud enough.

"I'll rip up one of these cotton stalks and wear your tail out with it!! Did I ask you a question or what?"

My response, of course, was much louder this time. But the last thing I was expecting was a whipping. Yet I was on the very verge of getting one.

"Aw, come on," my mother said from the distance! "Don't be so hard on him, Edmond. After all, it is his first day, you know."

"You stay out of this, Magnolia, dog-bite-your-picture! You stay out of this," my father gruffed!

But she kept on talking as if my father hadn't said a word. "He's got to get the hang of this thing just like the rest of us, including you. But I guess you done got too old to remember." Both my mom's sarcasm and interference got next to my father who was now angrier at her than he was with me. And that's when I realize I had let my father down.

My father's hopes of undermining Jessie Mae's dominance were suddenly headed down the drain. And he was becoming more and more disappointed with me due to my inability to adapt, a flaw he'd discovered in all my male predecessors. Up until this very day, he'd harbored the notion that I'd be the one to subdue the high-strung girl, that I'd become her male counterpart. Yet instead, I'd proved to be just another of his

113

mediocre offspring. So almost immediately, he developed a habit of taking his frustrations out on me.

Deep within his soul, he knew Mr. Miles cheated him out of every dime he hadn't borrowed. And the size of his family was the only reason the old goat, who otherwise wouldn't have had the slightest use for him, favored him. There were other sharecroppers who periodically courted my father for the same reason. The size of his family was his greatest asset. Yet other than Jessie Mae, not a single one of us showed the slightest interest in picking cotton. But he'd always harbored the notion that this one would be different. But here he was watching his demented dreams crumble right before his eyes. And this was the first time I saw that something in my father's eyes, which I knew would take a lifetime to overthrow.

He looked disdainfully down upon me and said, "I thought you were gonna be something special. But all I see now is nothing but a lousy excuse for a human being."

But since she'd never heard him address the other children in such a manner, my mother - who resented the remark - straightened up.

But he refused her a chance to speak. "Ain't this a mess," he said as if trying to shame my mother?! "You'd rather take this boy's side than mine. Well you done got the rest of them to where they ain't worth a damn, Magnolia. But not this one, Magnolia - not this one! This one is gonna learn to pull his weight around here. So you can just keep your ill-advised opinions to your self!"

114

To which she complied.

And then, a long period of silence ensued which, in time, I'd come to realize was quite normal out here. But by then, I'd fallen so far behind until I became disgusted. So I began to wail. I wailed until I heard my father coming back again. "C'mon," he shouted! "You got to do better than this!"

And the next thing I heard was rustling through the bushes after which he emerged with a distorted face.

"What you doing" he asked? "Boy you got the nerve to be crying? Is you done lost your mind or what? I can't believe this!"

"I want to go home," I said!

"YOU WHAT?!! I'll show you where you're going alright," he said, reaching for a huge cotton stalk, which he yanked up and ripped the limbs from. I jumped up and started hustling to get my sack back on.

"You see this switch?" He said.

"Yassir."

"Well I'm gonna catch you up one more time! And if you don't keep up from now on, I'm gonna take this switch and wear your tail out with it. YOU Hear?!!!"

"Yassir!"

"And by the time we finish, I want to see enough cotton in that sack to weigh in at the scale tonight. Otherwise,

I'm wearing your butt out!"

He was angry yet I was tired - as if I'd done three days work - and was wishing I'd slept the night before instead of lamenting over such a rotten situation as this. Not simply tired, but hungry and angry at myself for conjuring up so many silly dreams. My stomach growled for the breakfast I'd missed. So in order to ease the pain, I started picking harder and faster. Yet my sack acted as if it had a hole in it. It seemed the harder I picked the less cotton the thing contained. Even more disappointing was the fact that while I was struggling to reach the halfway point, Jessie Mae was headed back in the opposite direction. Every muscle and bone within me ached and I had never been so miserable before.

So 'why,' I asked myself, 'was the one thing I'd always thought I wanted to do turning out to be the worst thing I could've imagined?' The part that hurt most was I immediately knew it was something I'd never be able to adapt to. So starting that day, I contemplated running away. I'm only six years-old but I'm thinking the most logical way to deal with this situation was to run away which I most certainly would someday.

I picked sixteen pounds and, in subsequent days, prayed for rain. But the clouds dawdled with my mind. Yet it was the simple hope for rain that gave me the strength to make it through yet another day.

CHAPTER 29 "BACK AND FORTH"

In two years time, my dad demanded a hundred pounds a day and not a pound less, something I could never come up with. Yet every time I failed, he whipped me viciously. I'd always start out giving it my best. But by mid-day I'd grow weary. I picked 88 pounds, 89 pounds, 92 pounds and often as much as 98 pounds. But none of these satisfied my father.

It was as if he'd developed a revulsion for me and I'd actually became his sounding board - a tool to douse his own sense of defeat. Anytime he was having a bad day, my ass had to pay. It was that simple. He didn't care what he whipped me with - either an ironing cord, a wet or a dry rope, a huge cotton stalk or an occasional wire hanger. You'd think I would have developed a tolerance for pain but I never did. Instead, I developed an equal distaste for my very own father.

Throughout the ensuing years, however, I learned of the huge tower of pressure hanging over his head, and realized how he was taking out on my behind the equivalence of what Mr. Miles was taking out on his mind - an unfair exchange yet somewhat of a logical conclusion. Whether my dad knew it or not, he'd settled for a diverse form of slavery. For day in and day out, he worked us like animals. Yet without failure, Mr. Miles cheated him out of every cent he thought he had coming. It was the same every year, one excuse after another, which forced my father to borrow money to pay back money he'd already borrowed. From the very day he became involved with the shyster, he'd fallen into a pit of defoliation, which my mother strived to bring to his attention.

He practically lived in a state of denial and had long since lost sight of the forest for the trees. But still he knew he had money coming, but as long as The Triple B System was in effect, neither he nor his contemporaries stood a chance of collecting any. Yet no matter how many times my mom told him he was spinning his wheels, he, like the rest, perpetually tried to convince the old charlatan that he was an honorable citizen.

He did eventually take my mother's advice and accepted an offer from the old man's staunchest competitor. A man named Jack Crawford who offered Dad $600 in advance which was more money than he'd ever seen in his entire life.

We moved out in the middle of night and into a house twice the size of the shotgun shack Mr. Miles had provided. It had a thriving orchard, which stretched at least 300 feet beyond the house with fruit trees galore. The house also had a defunct smoke house where little scorpions ran back and forth between it and the main structure. My dad found himself in a worse situation here, though. For besides the $600, which he squandered almost immediately, this sharecropper-come-slave- driver wouldn't allow enough money to make it through the winter or to buy toys for Christmas. What he did in fact was to give us the hand-me-downs his children had wore out before we obtained them. He conveniently forgot to tell my dad until we were well settled in that the orchard was exempt from his use except for once some cannery or another collected the prime fruits.

My dad still owed $400 of the $600 by the end of the second year. And beyond that, we were required to work 55 acres of tough bottomland as opposed to the 40 acres we were accustomed to. And from the very day we moved in, old man Miles came a-courting my father to come back and work for him. But since he'd taken Mr. Crawford's money, he felt obligated to prove to this white man as well that he was honorable.

But there was a mouse in the house and it was driving Dorothy Jean, the last-born child, up the wall. She had a genuine phobia for the thing which was a common house mouse but which she referred to as "DAT WAT!" The first time she saw it, it came dashing out of its cubbyhole in broad daylight and it frightened her out of her wits. The hole appeared much too small for the creature yet it squeezed in and out with the utmost agility.

Since she'd never seen it before, she was quite traumatized which the creature must've sensed because it leaned and dashed directly beneath the bed she was laying in. She unleashed the loudest scream her lungs could discharge causing the rodent to come out from under the bed and my mother to come a-rushing in to see what was going on. And quite to her surprise, my mother discovered her most unexcitable child gasping for air. So she snatched the child up to make sure it wasn't bit by an ant or a spider, or stung by a scorpion. Yet she found no unusual marks. So she finally locked on to Dorothy Jean's finger, which pointed towards a hole in the wall that, up until then, had little or no significance. But the mouse stuck his head out the cubbyhole and exposed its whiskers.

"Aw, honey," said Mom. "That ain't nothing but an ole' rat."

But regardless of how unimportant my mom tried to make it appear, Dorothy Jean didn't relish being in the same room with it. And though my mother tried to calm her down, she never lowered her voice until she was removed from the room. My mother eventually rocked her back to sleep and took her back into the room where she woke up and refused to sleep in there again. Then mother, who didn't particularly like the predicament, told my father if he didn't do something, she and her female children were gonna move out. It was a typical threat but was enough to force my father to seal up the hole. But even this did little to deter Dorothy Jean who saw the thing even when it wasn't there.

"That WAT," she declared! "It's in my shoe! That wat's in my soup!" The girl imagined the thing practically everywhere.

And for quite some time, my father complained of her kicking and accused her of stopping the flow of babies into the Wright household. But the girl was the apple of mom's eye so it didn't matter how much he complained. The child would have her way. And in fact, it was she who provided the excuse for us to move back into The Triple B trap.

120

This time, however, he gave us an "L" shaped facility, which provided more space, but the prevalence was the same. By his very nature, Mr. Miles was a sadist who held a pow-wow with Mr. Crawford whom he told there was no way my father owed $400 when he left there. He'd interrogated my father and knew how much cotton we'd picked.

He also knew how much cotton sold for that year. And had Mr. Crawford treated my father fairly, he would've left there with at least a thousand dollars in his pockets.

"You may be able to bullshit one of my nigras," he told the man. "But you'd have to get up pretty early in the morning to pull one over on me."

The two men parted with a handshake after which Mr. Miles told Dad the debt was taken care of. At which time he revealed that he was going to take the money out of each settlement, which threw my dad, right back into his debt. Then he pulled out of the yard, a smile unraveling his furrowed features, and was feeling quite full of himself. For, he'd killed two birds with one stone. Not simply was he guaranteed four more years of loyal service but Mom was pregnant and yet another set of hands would soon be added to the fray.

According to Mr. Miles, however - come settlement time - my dad was so deep into his debt until he could only allow $50 for the winter.

"Fifty dollars," complained my father, but sorry is all he got.

"So better luck next time," he said.

"But Mr. Miles," pleaded Dad. "I don't see how we can make it on this."

"Sorry," said Mr. Miles. "But since you're so far behind that's about the best I can do. But I've got good news, though! They tell me next year's crop is gonna be a doozy, at least according to my Almanac. And the price of cotton is gonna shoot sky high. So I can just about guarantee you we're gonna make a killing next year!"

Then he took off and left my father in yet another luminous cloud of dust.

CHAPTER 30   "AUNT SISSY'S JUMPING JUKE JOINT"

Now three years passed since McClain shot and killed Bill, and so many changes had taken place. Mom sent Inez off to school for three years, but she only stayed two and was presently running with my mom's sister Sissy, who ran the local juke joint. Neither Mom nor Dad associated with her sister anymore, for according to the Bible and my father's interpretation of it, she lived a hedonistic existence. Yet the only thing wrong with Aunt Sissy was she liked having fun. So for this reason, at least in my father's mind, she was among the lowest of the low. She was 32 and had been married three times which, for this reason, my dad wouldn't allow my mom to associate with her.

No one in the household was allowed to so much as peek into aunt Sissy's Juke Joint, for to do so was punishable by God Himself. That's if my father didn't get to you first. There was a sort of logic to my parents' madness, for some poor individual was injured or mortally wounded practically on a weekly basis in her joint. Which was the reason my parents referred to it as a weeding out factory for Negroes. They often spoke in jest but what actually failed to be funny was the vast number of people who got away with murder there. It seemed every murderous tale had the same ring to it. For instance, if one of Mr. Miles' sharecroppers killed another from let's say Joe Adams' plantation, Miles' son would bail him out in time for work on Monday morning and vice versa. If the family became hostile towards the killer, his boss would have him sent out of state until everything cooled down.

But the price for the killer was for the rest of his entire life, at the mercy of his benefactor. So should he ever get out of line, his boss could have him both arrested and tried for murder. This, as far as I was concerned, was one of the lowest forms of slavery and, certainly, was nothing to laugh at. I also found no comedy in the fact that those who flocked to my Aunt's joint were subjecting themselves to a dangerous situation. And 'what,' I wondered, 'could possibly possess a person to go there?' But then one Friday afternoon, my father left me in his car and went into the store, which was the first time I'd heard blues music emanating from my Aunt's Juke Joint.

Someone was playing this haunting melody by Sonny Boy Williamson, which they played over and over. "Keep Our Secret to Ourselves" was the theme as Sonny Boy cautioned his lover,

"You've got a husband and I've got a wife / You start talking now baby and you gonna mess up both our lives / So please, baby, please / Please keep our secrets to yourself"

Sissy's Joint was the only place except True Vine Baptist Church where black people could go to release tensions. And since both places used music as their primary ritual, what a better way, I thought - other than musical therapy - for a person to release pent-up tensions. The song typified the sort of infidelity that often took place in the rural south, and it also typified the reason some

124

people lost their lives in such a rude manner in such a place.

The blues was something I rarely heard except for the few times I heard Muddy Waters rehearse across the street from my grandma's house. Yet I understood both pain and suffering. But still it was beyond me to comprehend why people lost so much love for themselves and each other. So much until, they seemed to be willing to kill those who resemble them the most. Those who kill people, who resemble themselves, I reasoned, were not very far removed from a willingness to destroy their very own souls. So after witnessing the unpleasant death of Bill Williams, I developed an aversion for all unnecessary waste of life.

I was therefore reminded of how the living conditions among the Mississippi slave hands had the propensity to drive an entire race of people into a state of neurosis. And though not fully aware of it, I, too, had fallen under the spell of Aunt Sissy's jukebox. So as I sat there pondering these things, it drew upon me insistently, the repetitious song practically overtook my mind. And so, unbeknownst to myself, my head was bobbing and I was patting my feet and going through all sorts of physical gyrations, and was releasing the pain and frustration which had long since built up within me.

But suddenly, my dad walked up and slapped the pure d shit out of me! It was such a surprise until an infectious howl, which spread across the countryside came a-jutting up from my lungs. And no sooner than we arrived home as a further punishment, my father wouldn't allow me so much as a crumb of bread for my super that night.

CHAPTER 31 "JUST BELOW THE SURFACE"

Three years after the tragic incident with Bill Williams, McClain returned on a pitch-black night. And being that she was so overwhelmed, my mother broke out in tears. So I ventured into my parents' room, only to see my brother crouched over the bed.

"My God," he said. "Boy, c'mon over here and let me take a good look at you."

But I was shocked to see his hands had blotches on them as pink as Mr. Miles, and even whiter in spots. His face was inundated with them.

So, "Hello," I said, approaching him cautiously, hiding my emotions.

"Come on over here," said my brother, "and let me take a good look at you!"

He grabbed me and flung me around several times.

"Boy," he said, "you certainly have grown since I've seen you. So what y'all been feeding him anyway? And where is Jessie Mae and Edna Rea?"

I said "They're there in the room."

"Now, what's this," he asked peering over into the bed? "Is that what I think it is?"

"It certainly is," said my father. "This is your newest sister, Doris Ann."

"Oh! So let me see," said McClain as he reached over and picked the baby up.

"Boy, you sure look good," said my father. "Like the picture of health itself."

"Well, thank you," said McClain but he knew my father was lying. "Yessiree," said my brother. "I've had some pretty rough times, you know."

"Well, if you don't mind me asking," said Dad, "what in the world happened to you anyway?"

"Well," said my brother. "After I left here, I landed a job as a cook in the Memphis train station. I was cooking breakfast one morning, and a huge pot of grits exploded in my face. It burnt the entire upper part of my body. And the doctors didn't know for the longest, if I was gonna' make it. In fact, I didn't know either. But here I am, thank God Almighty."

"Boy, you is blessed! And you sound like you meant it, too."

"What's that?"

"'Thank God Almighty' and all."

"Oh, Daddy, a whole lot has happened since I left here! I know you won't believe it but I have accepted Jesus Christ as my Lord and Savior who enlightened me to go unto the multitude and preach His Word."

"YOU WHAT? Oh, my God," said my father! "What a blessing!"

128

Then Mom cut in, "But I'm afraid I have some distressing news. It appears the United States Government has other plans for you."

"The Government," asked my brother? "What in the world would the government want with me?"

"Go over to the shift row and look in that second drawer for a brown envelope."

McClain got up with a concerned expression and sifted through the junk until he came upon the envelope. After he opened the thing, he said, "Oh, my God. This was six months ago. I'd better hurry up. Otherwise, there just might be consequences."

"Since it's been so long," said my mother, "it's altogether possible they'll forget the whole thing."

"Don't go getting this boy's hopes up for nothing," said my father. "I suggest you go in to town first thing in the morning so you can see what this is about."

My dad crawled out of bed and got down on his knees. "God only knows," he said, "how to deal with this sort of a situation. So let us pray."

We all knelt down on our knees and when we finished, mom got up and lit the wood-burning stove. She cooked breakfast for us all that morning but catered to McClain who must've earned a Ph.D. in flattery since he was away - and especially to women about their culinary attributes.

He raised one of Mom's biscuits just above eye level and

said, "There ain't a biscuit this good in the entire state of Tennessee!"

My mother, meanwhile, was bouncing around the kitchen like a teenager. And the more he bragged, the more food she piled up on his plate. My father didn't mind McClain's bragging yet he was not happy with how he was using his skills to manipulate our mother.

So before he knew it, the words flew out. "I'll be doggone," he exclaimed! "I guess I don't deserve no consideration around here anymore, especially since this boy done come in here and took over."

"Oh, my Lord, I'm sorry," said Mom! "I done messed around and done exactly what I didn't want to do. Honey I'm so sorry, but it's been almost three years since I've seen my child."

"But he ain't the only one here and he certainly ain't the only one who enjoys your cooking," said Dad. Otherwise, I'd-a long since been gone!"

There was one thing my mom knew for sure. There is no one on the planet who could mess a situation up, better than my dad. So she immediately gave him all the attention she thought he needed.

McClain got up the next morning and went into Clarksdale only to find he had no choice but to join the Army. He figured on staying close at hand so he could be near the family. They'd given him six weeks to get his business in order. So he decided to try and make amends with the Williams family, which he did, except

130

for with Clyde.

Clyde eased up on him at the drug store in Clarksdale one night and propositioned McClain to take him to where he'd left his truck the night before. My brother asked where he'd left it to which Clyde said he left it over on Church Lane. Church Lane was a place where fellows took red-hot women in the middle of the night but it had yet another significance. It was also adjacent to the same cemetery where Clyde was shooting at him in the wake his brother's death.

So he told him, "I wouldn't mind taking you but I'd have to do it during daylight hours. And even then I'd have to bring someone with me."

Clyde looked at him with bloodshot eyes, called him a cowardly punk and then he wobbled out the doorway. He eventually moved to Chicago and was never seen again.

My brother McClain had a flair for talking, so he became a darn good preacher, which all the ladies in Clarksdale immediately took to and which gave him access to his choice among them. The entire family went to see him one Sunday. So the Saturday before that, my parents went and bought Frankie D. and me some new navy blue outfits. Little navy blue suits with white stripes and white caps.

We heard these two ladies talking when the service was over about McClain's preaching abilities. "Lord," said one. "That boy sure can preach."

"And to be so young," said the other one.

"He can preach for me any day of the week."

"You ain't said nothing honey. He can preach for me each and every day - and twice on Sundays."

"Well, he can park his shoes under my bed permanently," said the other one before they fell out laughing!

We heard other people talking about my brother's preaching abilities, too, but it was times like these when my mother's selfish side emerged. My father had taken her three kids in from her previous marriage and treated them as if they were his very own. But anytime my two stepbrothers from my father's side came over, she'd lose her patience immediately. And anytime my father did something that she didn't like towards hers, she'd go, "This is MY child! MY child! MY child!" And was the same way that Sunday when she thought McClain had done something great. She kept on, "MY child" this, "MY child" that..." And it eventually got next to my father, at which point he explained to her how she had changed since my brother re-arrived and it was not for the better. And since the statement was true, it brought out the preeminent evil within my mother.

She was very pissed off and she knew that my father's preaching ability was lacking. So she decided to use that as a weapon to defeat him. So she got behind my father, "You just jealous 'cause my son preached a great sermon, ain't you? And you wish it was you, don't you? I know you do Edmond, now don't you?"

My father finally became impatient but she got right behind him. He walked up the steps of the porch and she was right up on him, beating him down about his inability to preach.

She then mentioned Estelle. "Do you think she was attracted to you because of your preaching ability? Well, I got news. That ole' dog we got out there could preach a ring around your ass! You couldn't preach your way out of a paper bag!"

So, angry, my father turned and for the first time, I saw veins pop out on his forehead and his eyes dilated. He grabbed my mother and raised his fist. She was still kicking and scratching and beating him down with the most-vile language! But as he was about to strike her, you could see the fear in her eyes. It was as if she knew the huge fist was about to descend upon her!

But right before the blow was to fall, my father gathered the courage to nullify it. And all of us children who were on the very verge of tears suddenly had no reason to cry. They were now laying on the bed - my mother on her back and my father facing down upon her - looking dead into each other's eyes, laughing like two out of control lunatics. And oh, my God, what a rollercoaster ride...what a rollercoaster ride!

CHAPTER 32 "TOO BEAUTIFUL TO MARRY ON A WEEKDAY"

Our mother and father rarely allowed them selves to fight in front of us children. Yet there were matters they disagreed upon, such as the affair between McClain and Lula Mae McPherson.

My brother brought this fine, too-good-to-eat looking creature home one night whose beauty was so profound she neither needed nor wore makeup. The girl's hair hung below her waist like a silvery waterfall. And McClain, who couldn't keep his hands off her, continually snuggled up against her. He was happier then than I'd seen him since he killed Bill Williams. And my father, as he was for any good-looking woman, was like putty in Lula Mae's hands. Yet I suspect I'm the one who posed the greatest threat because I climbed up on her lap and practically refused to get down.

She seemed rather comfortable with me, too, and acted as if she didn't want me to get down. But when McClain was ready to leave, he politely asked me to move. Yet both she and I refused to cooperate. She squeezed me a little tighter, which indicated she didn't want me to dismount.

But my father intervened. "Boy, what's wrong with you," he asked? "Either you get down from there or I'm gonna take my belt off and wear your tail out with it!"

So to this harsh request, I slid down the "V" of the foxy girl's frame.

134

And after brushing the wrinkles from her skirt, McClain took a hold of her and just before they left said, "I think I'm in love for sure this time, Mama."

"And just how," asked Mom before he whisked her off, "does a person 'think for sure?'"

But ignoring her question, he snatched the girl through the doorway and whisked her off into the night.

And since my father was so ecstatic, my mom kept a-rolling her eyes across the ceiling.

"Now that," said my dad, "is one hell of a gal there. God sure is done blessed that boy this time around."

"Well I'll be doggone," said mother! "I can't believe you turned out to be such a pushover."

"Look who's jealous now," said my father.

"Jealous my butt," said my mother! "They call that a mother's intuition where I come from. She's good looking, all right, but good for what? Now that's the question. "McClain," she said. "He's about as big a pushover as you, especially when it comes to these women folk."

"Well now, why you want to come down on the boy like that," asked my father?

"Cause both you and Mack ought to know, you can't judge a book by its cover. And especially after all we've been through with these white folks down here."

"Aw c'mon Magnolia, even you have to admit that girl there is one more fine, super fine specimen of a woman-hood."

"Oh, she looks good Edmond but she smells of trouble. And I mean pure D trouble, too! And if you ask me, I'd say she actually reeks of it."

"Well, the boy is grown now," said my father. "So, whatever he's doing ain't none of our business - neither mine or yours."

My mother, even though she had an uneasy feeling about the girl, allowed the subject to drop - at least for the time being. Yet the feeling lingered on in back of her mind.

The next time McClain brought the girl by, to everyone's surprise, they'd just got married! My mama was outdone but what could she do? Reluctantly, she cooked dinner at McClain's request. McClain, meanwhile, went on and on about my mother's cooking. And by the time she was through, my mother decided to put her feelings aside. For knowing he was headed off to war she wanted my brother to extract all the pleasure he could out of his present situation. She had no idea what was in store for him. And God forbid he'd return wounded or, even worse, in a wooden box. Though my mother didn't like the girl - she actually hated her - she gained some satisfaction knowing that my brother was happy...at least for the time being.

On the third visit however, her suspicions began to collect dividends. The two of them had been arguing

136

long before they arrived and were still at each other's throats. Even my dad could see the girl was possessed and was not the sweet little innocent creature she originally appeared to be. She was constantly reminding my brother that she was her own person and was also accusing him of trying to make her into something she wasn't. My brother kept reminding her that she was a preacher's wife and she had to start acting like one. But to this she spewed a ghastly mouth, "Humph!" My parents, who'd held their breath, suddenly became unglued due to the girl's attitude.

So, "Now listen," said my father, who was actually my brother's stepfather. "Ain't nobody, except your mother and me going to argue in this house. So I suggest you take your wife someplace else to argue."

Anytime McClain came after that, he was alone. And on the day of his departure, mom cooked practically everything he wanted for his breakfast: fluffy biscuits with fig jam, scrambled eggs and a glass of milk...

And no sooner than he finished, all of us escorted him to the Mattson Train Depot. He was the only passenger to board the train that day where, usually, there were none. Gripping his suitcase, he waved until the train disappeared.

"Please, Lord," said Mom. "Protect him and send him back to me alive and well."

We all followed as she turned and walked off the platform.

"There he goes," she said, "my other prized possession. Sissy done took Inez lock stock and barrel. And only God knows what's next."

She looked back once again but the only reminder was dissipating smoke...and even that had all but disappeared. She took Grady, the only other child from her original marriage, by the hand and while struggling to hide her tears, they walked off ahead of us. She knew the train was taking a part of her further and further away while taking my brother closer and closer to a perilous situation – to fight for a cause, which neither he or my mother totally understood.

CHAPTER 33 "THE ARROGANT BLACK MULE"

Now Ole' Dan, which my father kept in a corral bound on one side by barbed wire that he built one summer during the drought, was the most incredible mule south of the Mason Dixon line. The fence was mostly submerged and was built in an oval shape. Yet anytime the intelligent mule got the urge, rarely was there a fence that could hold him. He'd jumped the fence on the road side or swim across on the waterside. It really didn't matter. For if mules had a motto, his would've certainly been, "You Can't Keep a Good Mule Down." The mule had a habit of going over the waterside after a storm, which he'd manage without so much as a scratch. And my dad actually admired the shiny black animal, which without a wagon or a plow hitched to its back, was more than a handful to handle.

I was merely 7 years-old, when my dad hooked up the wagon, then he put four empty barrels on it and he sent me to the gin to get drinking water. It was a welcome surprise for me since it was such a hot day amid chopping season. But as soon as I was out of sight, I disobeyed my father and raced his mule team. This time, however, when we reached the crossroads, Ole' Dan decided to make an abrupt turn instead of keeping straight.

'Who knows,' I'm sure he thought. 'We might lose the water barrels. But even better - this obstinate little pest who thinks he's the king of the road - maybe he'll fall off and break his stupid ass neck!'

So instead of turning the wagon completely over, the mules cut across Mr. Miles' prize cotton patch. I was quite taken by surprise when the wagon shifted beneath my feet but I'd been blessed with swift reflexes. So I grabbed the closest panel and, though it felt quite awkward, I continued to struggle until I brought the wagon to a complete halt. The other mule, Bob, seemed to be cooperating but 'Ole Dan kept a- bucking and a-romping... Yet somehow, I regained my footing, only to realize I was on the wrong road and the wagon was headed in the wrong direction. The only thing I had to control the mules with were the ropes I used to guide them. And both the mules and I knew I could not do much damage with those. So I spent a nominal amount of time trying to force them to move but Ole' Dan wouldn't budge.

I broke down after-while and started pleading with the mules, but Ole' Dan wasn't hearing it. He didn't like anyone beating him or trying to force him to do anything. And he wouldn't take that kind of abuse from anyone, let alone an inconsiderate pest such as myself. So being extra cautious, I climbed off the wagon thinking Ole' Dan could've been waiting for such an opportunity to disrupt more manicured cotton and possibly return home without me or the desperately needed water. My dad would've been furious! And I'd never get another chance to escape the grueling cotton patch.

So holding on to the ropes and moving cautiously,

"Whoa now," I repeated. "Whoa," I whispered. "Easy does it now, ok? Whoa, now! Whoa, boy!!"

I slowly rubbed my hand down Ole' Dan's elongated forehead. But he was agitated and so he simply jerked it up beyond my reach, as if saying, 'Take your filthy hands off me!' He then slowly eased his head down to the original position. So I tried to rub his forehead again but the mule duplicated the gesture. So I eased over to Bob's side and discovered he, too, was sweating profusely. It was then that I realized what my dad meant when he said, "Do not race my mule team!" I had therefore learned a lesson.

Yet the only lesson mules understood was the way in which you treated them. So how were they to know I'd finally come to my senses? Ole' Dan was fuming! So when I took a-hold of his bridle and tried to turn him around again, he simply raised his hoof and stomped it directly down upon my big toe, as if he was trying to say, 'This is for being such a stupid ass, empty headed little son-of-a-bitch!'

I clearly saw my own reflection in his huge eye and could detect the mule's bitterness as I grabbed a hold of my foot. The pain, which shot up my leg, reminded me of the incident with the axe. And the broken toe was a lesson, which I will endure the rest of my entire life - a reminder that no one should be cruel to animals, especially the domesticated kind.

No sooner than I got over the initial shock, I re-took control of the situation. And Ole' Dan simply turned the wagon around as ordered and got back on the path to

141

the gin. He proudly marched the rest of the way without the slightest provocation. And he never gave me another problem.

From that day forward, he and I shared a mutual respect for each other. But afraid I'd never be able to escape the cotton patch again, I never told a soul about my toe - of which I suffered in silence. In fact, I never mentioned it to anyone until this very day. You, therefore, are the first to know.

CHAPTER 34 "STONEWALL'S LETHAL CONCOCTION"

Stonewall Jackson was a big black potbellied man, who wore a black derby and was notorious for his ability to conjure up the spirits. His son drove him around in a huge black Hudson Tara plane automobile. He was also congenial enough to secure an ad in some national magazine or another, which drew people of all races and from all walks of life who came to seek his method of cure. They came from Tennessee, Oklahoma, Florida, Kentucky, Arkansas, Indianapolis, and as far away as New York City.

And had your wife threatened to leave you or your sexual organs failed, Stonewall had the cure! If you'd been searching for a long lost lover or suffered from a rare disease, it was Stonewall to the rescue! He was famous for his strange tasting brews and medicines from his herb garden from which he created all sorts of concoctions, many of which were beyond the scope of modern medicine. Stonewall was a rare species as far as black people went for he didn't have to raise cotton for a living nor was he apt to do anything that was illegal. He simply engaged his mind and his odd looks to support his family in an affectionate way.

Apart from his herb garden, Stonewall raised one of the healthiest fields of corn in the entire state. But the first thing Ole' Dan did upon his frequent escapes was to raid Stonewall's corn patch.

So expressing a growing intolerance for the mule's

behavior, he took the liberty to tell my dad, "If your mule insists on raiding my corn patch, I'm gonna turn a flock of little demons a-loose on him!"

And sure enough in the fall of '46, 'Ole Dan came back carrying on in the strangest manner. The mule had taken on a horrific ailment, which he suffered from for the better part of a week. Whatever it was he'd ingested was eating him from within and, by the third day, it was doubtful that he'd survive.

My father had no proof but suspected Stonewall poisoned the once formidable mule. Ole' Dan eventually lay down on a stack of hay where my dad rubbed him down with liniment and force-fed him homemade concoctions. Subsequently, he went into town and returned with a vet who looked at the mule and shook his head... My dad went back into town with the vet but by the time he returned, the mule had made its final transition.

Later on that day, a rusty colored semi-truck arrived with a tailgate slightly taller than its side panels. The thing was endowed with several winches. The tailgate had its own winch, which, after easing down to the ground, functioned as a ramp. And slightly before it reached the ground, the operator dawned himself with thick gloves then took a hold of a metal rope and turned yet another winch on. He then started pulling the rope towards Ole' Dan's stiffened head. He'd already backed the truck up to within feet of his lifeless body. So he eventually took the looped end of the rope and lifted Ole' Dan's head, then slipped the noose around it after which he walked back to the truck and reversed the winch.

With broken hearts, Frankie D. and I, watched as the unbreakable mule was slowly drug through the manure, laden dust. Finally when it reached the tailgate, it lurched several times and was eventually placed next to several other dead animals.

Only one day in my life could I remember feeling so low - it was the day a rabid dog came along and bit our dog, Buster. So dad took the unsuspecting creature for a walk then as soon as they cleared the shack, he spun around and blew Buster's head to bits with his shotgun. Grady and James Lee took the dog's remains into the woods where they left it for buzzard's meat. Yet two days later, the loyal creature returned with one of his eyeballs dragging the floor. We all begged Daddy to please keep the dog and to try and fix its eye but he knew he couldn't. So again he fetched his shotgun and again he walked out the door. "Come on, boy. Come on, Buster," he said. "Come on, now."

We were all hoping the dog would disobey and run away but he was such a loyal creature, he followed my dad to the very same spot where he spun around and blew what was left of his obedient head completely off.

'How cruel,' I thought, 'could anyone be, let alone my very own father!' I was too young and didn't understand how he was doing this to protect the safety of his entire family.

The driver climbed up the side and placed two pins at

145

the top of the tailgate. Then quite to my surprise, he thanked my father for 'Ole Dan's remains!

"And exactly what," I asked him, "do you intend to do with our mule?"

"Well," said the driver looking down upon me amusingly, "we're gonna make bubble gum out of the lots of 'em, son."

I didn't know if the driver was serious or not, but right there and then I had learned an important lesson. Life, I learned, like everything else, twitters between positive and negative forces...but sometimes, you just don't know which one is which?

CHAPTER 35 "THE INDISCRIMINATE PIGS"

Shortly after 'Ole Dan's demise, my father moved the stable from the bayou to a shady spot on the opposite side of the shack. So I approached my father about turning the stable into a garden as a memorial to 'Ole Dan. I thought maybe I could breathe life back into the soil. And once he heard this, an old sparkle rejuvenated in his eyes. At least it did momentarily. He told me if I, was serious, he'd have one of the older boys to plow the plot up which he did.

Now from the outset, I knew the aspects of becoming a field hand bend you over, rob you of your identity and sap the life out of once vital individuals.

I was so glad to have this little slice of land, which wasn't simply a garden. It was a refuge unto itself. I loved strolling along the bayou, listening to the purest form of music in all God's creation. Crickets twittered, birds chirped, frogs croaked while woodpeckers pecked their nests in the highest trees. To me, this was a glorious thing. So I grew watermelons, cantaloupes, green beans, black-eyed peas and sweet potatoes. I grew some of the biggest pumpkins I've ever seen. But, as usual, my family preferred sweet potato pies. But the pigs, they were not so discriminating. The pigs; they ate pumpkins by the pound.

148

CHAPTER 36 "FOR HIS OWN SAKE"

On New Years Eve of '47, a severe winter storm swept across the fields, gripping them as would the talons of an angry eagle. And during its devastation, I developed snow blindness, which no one knew the slightest details of. So the only thing I could do was lay down on the floor and pray the blinding snow would go away. My condition was so critical until, during daylight hours, I dared not open my eyes for the slightest moment. For it was punishable by the most excruciating pain. And it felt as though cruel streaks of lightening were shooting into my brain.

But by mid-March, the sun broke through, rendering a subtle resolve as icicles fell from the L-shaped roof and splashed against the ground. The vast blanket of snow, which had concealed the ground for weeks, finally gave way to hardened patches and muddy ice puddles.

While swinging an axe over a knotty log, my father heard a distant motor straining. He looked up and saw an automobile towing something behind it but couldn't discern exactly what it was. Eventually, a trailer filled with used furniture and pots and pans materialized behind a car full of white folk. It soon passed and stopped at the shack less than a quarter of a mile away. Six children and two adults, all of whom appeared to be happy to find a place to call home, sprang from the vehicle.

These, were a different breed of white folk whose hair hung over their eyes like sheepdogs. And among the children were three plump girls, two others that appeared underfed, and one skinny boy. We'd seen white sharecroppers but never expected to live so close.

Shortly after they moved in, the first school bus we ever saw came a-bouncing up the gravel road. It picked them up in front of their shack and always dropped them off in front of Mr. Miles' mansion where they'd walk the rest of the way home.

They passed one afternoon while I was chopping wood. And I was attending school myself then which was quite rare. The teacher had taught us a song by Steven Foster, Jr. which I was proudly whistling as I chopped my blues away. I was whistling the haunting melody to "Beautiful Dreamer" and saw them as they passed. Yet I continued whistling until long after they'd faded into the distance. I whistled my way through the ordeal of taking the wood inside where my father ordered me to shut it down.

The following day, our family was working in the outer perimeters of the cotton patch when we heard the new neighbors picking in the adjacent field. By late afternoon, a slender figure emerged from between the cotton stalks and simply stood there, peering at us through his mane.

"I'd like to speak to you in private," he told my father, who pulled his sack off and approached the man before the two of them went off into the distance. My father returned shortly, but his face was overwrought with tension. "I'm burning your tail up again," he said.

150

So taken quite by surprise I asked, "What did I do?"

"You know what you done-done," he said.

"So what," asked Mom, "did that old strange looking peckerwood want?"

"This here boy," my father said," "he's been whistling at that man's daughters!"

"WHAT," exclaimed my mom! "Don't you know them is white girls? So what on earth is wrong with you? Don't you know you can get yourself hung by the neck and, even worse, castrated until you bleed to death? Lord, what kind of fool is this we've got?"

I tried to speak up for myself in my own defense but...

"That's right," my mother said. "Wear his tail OUT tonight! Whip his butt for me as well as for his own sake. If you don't do it, I guarantee you these white folks are gonna kill 'em for sure!"

"That old peckerwood," said my dad. "He could be lying, you know," which was the rarest, assumption he'd ever made.

Mom spent a few seconds thinking. "You could be right," she said. "But-"

"Yeah, I know," said my father. "I've got to do this for this boy's own sake."

"If you don't, I'm gonna kill him myself," said Mom. "Cause these white folks ain't gonna have no mercy on him. And I mean none whatsoever."

My father waited until I fell asleep that night. And to assure I'd never do such a thing again, he whipped me with a wet rope. But as far as I was concerned, the lie the children told and the whipping my father administered were similar acts of cruelty.

CHAPTER 37 "DANCING IN THE COTTON PATCH"

It was spring again and flocks of birds followed as my father plowed his field. Mocking birds, badgered crows and other creatures ran amuck as Frankie D. and I took advantage of Mother Nature. The fields were soon planted and twice chopped, then dense pods burst open and exposed their essence. Amid this grand scheme, our family amounted to mere specks of a fly, wading through this immense landscape, ridding it of its whiteness.

After realizing he'd gain the same results from Frankie D. as his predecessors, my father decided against coaxing him into challenging Jessie Mae. Frankie D. was a docile child anyway, and had not the capacity to threaten the high-strung girl. And as usual, she was out in front of us all, followed by Mom and Dad, who were followed by James Lee and Grady. Edna Rea, who was two years older than me, was lagging behind them. Then here I come - looking into the sky, praying for a rainstorm.

And behind me was Frankie D., struggling to avoid my father's abusive tongue. The boy was under a verbal attack, which contained less fervor than my father used on the rest of us. And I suspect it was at that time my father realized no one in their right mind wanted to follow in his pathetic footsteps.

The August heat was dry and wearisome. And the mercury peaked at 104 in the shade. The heat was so overwhelming until, other than my father's meager threats, no one spoke a word. Then suddenly a nagging occurrence prompted my mother to shed her sack and distance herself from the rest of us. Once she got as far as she could manage, she grabbed her stomach and heaved forward, throwing up her entire breakfast. With teary eyes and wobbly legs, she eventually regained her composure, which prompted my dad to shed his sack and come to her aid. He then suggested she should take it easy for a while.

The children, meanwhile, picked her rows in hopes she'd soon recover. Dad watched over Mom as a referee would a wounded fighter, wondering if it was something she ate or was she being attacked by some sort of a pestilence. Since she was no stranger to these particular emotions, my mother was not sure of her condition.

But then suddenly, she was overcome by an urge to laugh, which erupted with an equal force from her diaphragm as her prior urge to regurgitate. And due to this sudden transformation, we were all quite perplexed. Just moments ago she appeared quite afflicted but now she was carrying on like someone who'd completely lost her mind. So we all shed our sacks and, with confused faces, we gathered around her. Since my father had witnessed the scenario time and time again, he understood when a potent desire to eat something chalky began tugging at my mother's innards.

"So honey," said my mom with a broad smile. "You think

you can you spare one of these boys to go up there to Brookings' store?"

"And just what for," my father asked? But then, "Of course," he said, "whatever you want, baby, you just ask for it."

"Believe it or not," she said, "I'm craving Faultless Starch. And if I don't get some, ain't no telling what I might do."

"Is you sure," asked my dad? "I mean, you wouldn't be putting me on would you?" This he said as he slowly shed his sack and approached her with his arms outstretched.

"And while you're at it," she said, "tell him to bring me a hunk of cheddar cheese." And no sooner than they were within reach, they embraced and practically melted into each other's arms.

Then, stroking my father's neck, "And guess what," said Mom?

They both drew back and said, "IT'S ANOTHER BOY!"

Save for Frankie D, I was the only expendable hand. So they sent me off to the store, which was an opportunity I was glad to accept. The rest of the family went back to work but they soon heard rustling in the sandy soil. Mom looked up but only to discover it was my dad with his arms raised, twirling in circles and laughing like a madman. Watching him in adulation, she shook her head.

"Edmond Wright," she said. "You is really some kind of a fool, ain't you? But I guess you already know that, don't you? Lord, Lord, Lord what kind of a fool is I done married?"

CHAPTER 38   "DOUBLE BUBBLE TROUBLE"

When I got to the store, Mr. Brookings was in a good mood for a change. He was standing between the gas pumps with a pleasant look on his face and a nozzle in his hand.

"Go on in there, boy," he said. "I'll be in, in a few minutes."

So I went into the store and walked around looking at general merchandise. I knew little colored boys weren't supposed to touch anything. Yet there was a new gum display, which no child in his right mind could've resisted. But, little did I know, it was tried, tested and spelled PURE D TROUBLE for a little black ass boy like myself. From the moment I walked in, I was confronted by the scent of the rack and its multiple colored packages.

So after walking two and a half miles in over 100-degree weather, my mouth was dry and I desperately wanted to taste that of which I smelt. But I had no money - not a single penny. All I had was a note from my father requesting a box of starch and two pounds of cheese. Yet if the fragrance surrounding the rack was an indication of its product, Heaven had to have befallen Brookings' store that day. So once again I turned and walked past the gum rack, which made it seem even more irresistible. The next thing I knew, I was holding a package in my hand but, until then, I didn't realize what I was doing!

Then, from behind thick-rimmed glasses, I saw this withered expression of joy staring at me from beyond the store's front window. Shock waves emanated from my brain then spread throughout my heart, body and my soul, causing chills to go rushing up my spine. So in a feeble attempt to replace the one I held, I knocked over at least a dozen other packages then went scrambling to put them all back in place.

So no sooner than the storekeeper finished, he and his customer came into the store acting as if he hadn't seen a thing. 'So maybe, just maybe,' I thought, 'he hadn't.' So I breathed a deep sigh of relief.

The storekeeper, meanwhile, and his white customer were carrying on a pleasant conversation, which made me feel as though everything was quite copasetic. So after his customer left, he read the note, put the starch and the cheese into a #2 paper bag, and sent me on my way.

'WHEW,' I thought, as I was leaving, while praying I'd never have to go there again. It was quite a frightening situation since my parents always taught me:

Simply thinking of committing a crime is as bad as committing the crime itself.

CHAPTER 39   "PERCY"

Strong but void of personality, Ole' Dan's replacement was an awkward creature named Percy. And for some reason, Grady liked the clumsy mule, which was red in color and had a gait like that of an animated elephant. But as far as I was concerned, Percy was nothing but a waste of time.

Grady rode the mule to the store one day and came back with a personal note to my father. I could see my father's blood pressure rise as he read it. After which he looked down at me and he asked, "What did you do up there at Brookings' store the other day?"

"Nothing," I said with an innocent expression.

"Well then why do you think he wants me to bring you up there?" That's when the bubble gum incident suddenly slapped me dead upside the head!

I bucked my eyes and shrugged my shoulders, but he knew something was wrong.

"Whatever it is," he said, "I'm taking you up there to see what this is about."

"So," my mother asked after he finished, "What did that ole' honky want anyhow? You know he's been beating up little colored boys lately, don't you? Got a hold of Roosevelt Spencer the other day and practically killed the child."

"Well," said my father, "them ain't my boys and I ain't

got nothing to do with that, but this one is. So I'm taking him up there to see what this is all about."

"Well, I'm holding you responsible then," said Mom. "Don't you let nothing happen to my child up there, Edmond. Don't you let that crazy ass peckerwood touch a hair on his head! Why would you take your own child to slaughter anyhow," she asked?

But my father ignored her.

I was wishing it was yesterday, tomorrow or any other day except today as my daddy put me on the wagon to take me to the store. But upon our arrival, there was another customer so Mr. Brookings wasn't paying us any attention.

And once his customer left, "So how are you today, Mr. Brookings," my father said? But, still writing in his notebook, he didn't say a word. And all I could hear was a portable fan blowing throughout the store.

Finally, he looked up and said, "Oh, I see you brought this little 'ole buck-eyed coon to see me, eh." Then he pulled a strap from beneath his counter, which was four inches wide with suction holes. "I'm gonna wear his ass out with this here strap," he said, "which I keeping around for just such a purpose!"

"YOU WHAT," my father asked?

"I'm gonna wear his ass out for what he done-done. You know what you done-done, don't you boy? Is you got an ass licking coming or what," the storekeeper said looking down at me?

160

I was standing there about to urinate on myself. I was so afraid I could hardly speak.

"What's this about," asked my father?

"He tried to steal a piece of my bubble gum the other day."

"He did what," asked my father? He then looked down at me and then back at Mr. Brookings.

"That's why I'm wearing his ass out," he said.

"Wait a cotton-picking minute here," my dad said, trying to play on the old man's conscience. "You mean to tell me you had me to bring my child up here so you could whip him right in front of my face?"

"That's exactly what I had in mind," said Mr. Brookings. "Is you got a problem with that?"

"If he did something wrong," said my father, "I'm gonna whip him myself. I'll take him home and I'll wear his tail out."

"Aw hell naw, you're lying," said Brookings. "In that case, take this strap and whip his ass right here and right now."

"I'm sorry," said my dad. "I give you white folks all the respect you deserve. But I'm sorry sir, I can't let you whip my child."

"My parents," said Mr. Brookings, "they used to leave me with an old colored man. And anytime I got out of line,

161

he'd wear my ass out! And I mean he wore my natural ass out! So I think it's only fair for me to get an honest shot at this little black ass coon's ass, as well."

But to both my father's surprise and my delight, someone pulled up to the gas pump, which robbed the old man's scheme of its potency. Still he reiterated as he peered out the window, "If you don't let me whip this coon's ass, you won't get another ounce of credit from my establishment. Everything and I mean everything will be cash and carry from now on, you understand?"

He then straightened up and made a final gesture towards the door. My father snatched me out of the store, threw me up on the wagon and started talking about how he was gonna tear into my behind once he got me home.

"But I didn't do nothing."

"Well, this whipping," my father said, "is to ensure that you will never think of stealing anyone's property again for as long as you live." "But I didn't steal anything Daddy."

163

CHAPTER 40 "FETCH ME A SWITCH"

No sooner than we got home, my father told me to go fetch him a switch. So I went and I got the flimsiest thing I could find. He sent me for another. But the third time, he went and returned stripping limbs from a huge cotton stalk. A single look at the thing and I come to just a-begging.

So he asked, "Did you touch that bubble gum rack?"

"Yes sir," I said. "But-"

He instantly became furious and instructed me to take my pants off, which was a rare request. So I looked at the switch and thought, 'I don't think I can handle this with my clothes on.' I also knew running from my dad was suicidal. But I'd already made him repeat himself, which was another no-no. So I decided to take a chance.

But just as I exited the doorway, my sister Jessie Mae - who was already there, eavesdropping - stuck her bony leg out and tripped me. I fell on my face, which busted my lips. But the next thing I knew, my father had me by the arm.

"Do you think," he said, "you can RUN from me?" His first lick came down after the word "ME."

I had no idea how many times he struck me after that but made sure he saw the blood from my lips which was dripping all over the place. But that did me no good whatsoever. I suppose I raised such a ruckus until my mother decided to come inside. She noticed the blood

164

but, most importantly, the look on my father's face, which was as if he'd completely lost his mind.

So she did something that day she'd never done before or since. "Ok now," she said. "Now honey that's enough, ok? This has gone far enough, ok?"

But why did she say that? He bore down even harder than he had before. But again she repeated, "This has gone far enough!"

Yet each time she spoke up, the harder he bore down. He finally dropped me to the floor and said with his switch raised, "You must want some of this your goddamn self," he said!

My mother knew there was an unwritten law where neither of them was supposed to interrupt while the other one whipped a child. But this time she saw something within my father's eyes, which was quite unusual.

So, "Just go ahead," she said. "Anytime you feel froggish, you cockeyed son of a bitch, you just jump, okay?"

My father threw the switch to the floor and stormed out the shack and wasn't seen until later. And as a further punishment, he didn't say a word to my mother for at least a week, a method, which obviously worked because she never interrupted another of my father's vicious whippings.

166

CHAPTER 41 "A DAY LATE, A DOLLAR SHORT"

After slipping deeper and deeper into the abyss, my parents decided it was high time to get out of The Triple B System. And my father finally realized that if he continued to allow himself to be kicked around, he'd never amount to much - a conclusion he hadn't come to without a few hefty nudges.

But since old man Brookings once again refused to extend credit, my father was forced to do business at Mr. Dan's store in north Mattson. So while shopping there one day, he ran into Mr. Crawford again who propositioned him to come back and work for him under slightly different circumstances. He offered my father $200 this time and promised to forget the four hundred he left owing him. But, of course, my dad told the man he was under the impression that Mr. Miles had taken care of that debt. But after researching the fact, he realized the old man hadn't, regardless of the fact he'd taken money out of their last two settlements. Not simply that, he was threatening to take more out of subsequent settlements.

This brought about a bitter taste for the old shyster who'd introduced them to Christian ethics and now earned their ultimate scorn. After twenty-three years of slaves-man-ship, neither of my parents could stand the sight of the shyster anymore. So they decided as soon as possible to make an expedient departure. And after watching their white neighbors splurge, they figured the old man must've owed them a fortune. So Mom suggested getting at least some satisfaction while abandoning the situation. They owed, among other debts, a portion of the down payment on the last car dad purchased, but knowing there was no way to satisfy that. And even if they had, he'd find another way to snag them. They'd be stuck in the same perpetual rut for years trying to pay off his bogus debts.

My father's disposition was never to allow him self to do anything fraudulent. So he agreed to allow my mother the privilege of planning their escape. She'd never liked the old shyster and was more than willing to deal with the situation - and in somewhat of a devious manner. So after giving the predicament considerable thought and pondering my father's reaction, she divulged her plan one sunny afternoon.

"This man, my Mom said, "done mistreated us for so long, so why don't we get some satisfaction out of him for a change?"

But not knowing what to expect, she bent over and started picking while awaiting my dad's response. The only thing she was sure of was he was capable of changing his mind and especially when it had to do with Mr. Miles. But should he demonstrate such a weakness this time, she'd leave him for good. Yet to my mother's surprise my dad stood up displaying a mischievous grin.

"Now, you know good and well God don't like ugly, don't you?"

"I know," said Mom, "but don't the Good Book say an eye

168

for an eye and a tooth for a tooth?"

"I guess it does," said Dad. "So what's on that devilish mind of yours anyhow?"

My father's major drawback was he was passive and would avoid a ripple at any cost, and *especially* when he was dealing with white folks. So to confirm his status as such, "I never dreamt we'd be thinking of getting even with no white folks. So if you ask me Magnolia, I'd say we's about to do the devils work too, ain't we?"

"But that old man," said Mom, "he ain't nothing but the devil."

"I can't disagree," said Dad. "He definitely ain't no saint."

Unlike my dad, my mother - who was raised in Arkansas - was fortunate enough to gain a high school education. My dad, on the other hand, could barely spell his name.

Mom was at her wits end with the situation, so as if calling a bet or maybe even posing a threat, "Now you can act a fool and get to changing your mind if you want to," she said, "but not me, Edmond, not me!"

"Now just a doggone minute," said my father. "I ain't said nothing about changing my mind. But I ain't about to do nothing stupid either!"

No doubt, he still had the propensity to weaken but it was an option she could not afford. So she immediately asserted herself.

"So how much is that car worth," she asked?

"What car," asked my father?

"Our new neighbor's car, how much is it worth?" She'd already started figuring in her head.

"Oh, I guess about twelve to fifteen hundred dollars - so, why?"

"Just curious." "And how about that extra room they built?"

"That's a hard question," said my dad, "at least two to three hundred dollars. Why?"

"Umm-Huh! And what about that new barn they built?"

"Another hundred and fifty plus materials, so what is you getting at?"

Ignoring the question she sat down and started figuring in the dirt. And again she nodded towards the neighbor's place. "And how about that Ferguson tractor? How much you think that's worth?"

"I don't know, Magnolia. I don't have the slightest idea," said my dad, his eyes affixed on the thing. "Sure wish I had me one, though."

"Stop daydreaming, Edmond, and tell me what the thing is worth!"

"At least a thousand and eight hundred dollars," said Dad, "but I quite frankly do not know."

"That's alright," she said.

170

She then looked up with a bitter taste in her mouth yet a look of sweet discovery in her eyes - as if she'd finally seen the light!

"So how do you explain this," she asked? "They work twenty-five acres and come up with over three thousand in profits. And we work forty and end up owing this man a small fortune."

"My God," said Dad. "We can't win for losing!"

"We're over fifteen hundred in the hole without a dime to show for it!"

"I know that," said Dad." But I'm still trying to figure out exactly what's on your mind?"

"Well, I'm glad you asked," said Mom. "Cause I thought you never would."

My father was in a rare mood that day and, thus far, hadn't flown off the hook as he normally would. It's the best mood she'd seen him in since they were married. For since then, it seemed he'd traded his affection for her for his loyalty to old man Miles whom she resented for his propensity to kick my father around. Yet, she was happy to know my dad was finally showing an interest in abandoning their present situation. And since he hadn't maintained his usual posture of protecting the old rotten-toothed goat, my Mom figured she'd take advantage of the situation.

She'd been thinking of breaking away since Inez and Richard ran off to California. Inez, meanwhile, had bombarded her with scenic postcards of both Los

Angeles and Hollywood, which had aroused her curiosity. But my dad hadn't given anything so far-fetched the slightest notion. She, therefore, never shared her innermost thoughts with him.

CHAPTER 42 "A CHANCE TO EXPRESS HER SELF"

Finally, my mother figured she'd go out on a limb and, for once in her life, accept the consequences should she fail. Meanwhile, she had to be careful not to upset my father, in which case he'd shut down and she would have accomplished nothing. So she started out talking as if it should've normally been accepted.

"Now I've got this urge to go out to California and visit my daughter," said Mom. "She done already told me anytime I got ready she'd send me a round trip ticket. And that way anytime-"

"Now just a doggone minute," said my dad in the wake of his initial shock, "What in the devil's name is you talking about? You want to do WHAT?! Have you lost your mind, Magnolia? So what in the devil is that got to do with what we were talking about?"

"Please," begged Mom, "don't go flying off the hook for nothing. Can't you at least allow me to get the words out my mouth?"

"Because, as far as I'm concerned, what's coming out of your mouth ain't nothing but trash," said my father. "I never dreamt you'd be thinking of so much foolishness. Is you done lost your mind?"

"Now honey," Mom said in an attempt to cool him down. "I wouldn't think of doing anything without your approval and you know that. So why do you want to go flying all off the hook like that?"

"Well I'll be doggone," said my dad still in shock. "I don't know what you'll do anymore, Magnolia."

"Aw, come on, honey," said Mom. "Don't go getting bent all out of shape for nothing, "It's not like it's the end of the world, you know. It was just a suggestion. I ought to be able to make a suggestion, oughn't I?"

"Yeah, and I ought to be able to get upset, too," said Dad. "'Cause this mess that you're talking about is ridiculous! I done heard just about everything now. California," he repeated, "ain't this a mess?"

Since she'd done the opposite of what she intended and Dad's temperature had risen, she felt a rise of anticipation.

"I just wish you'd think about it," she added, "instead of going off again because I believe it's the best thing that could happen to either of us. But it won't be if you don't give me a chance to explain."

Since her train of thought was so far removed from his, my father knew - unless he allowed her to speak - he'd never know exactly what was on her mind. So he figured it'd be to his advantage to listen. "

Well," she said, "supposing you have a talk with that old goat and let him know if he don't start treating us better, we're gonna abandon this situation. Now, if my mind serves me right, he'll give you a positive response, but only if you make the proper approach. And if it makes you feel better, just put the blame on me. Tell

174

him I'm tired of living like a dog, I've had it up to HERE, and that I've long since been thinking of getting outta here! Plus, I refuse to pick another pound unless I see some drastic changes around here."

"But you know how mean that old man is, Magnolia. And this ain't gonna do nothing but make him even meaner. And the first thing he's gonna think is that I'm making a reference to them white folks down here. And you know good 'n well we ain't got no business comparing ourselves to no white folks."

"You don't have to mention those folks, honey, and especially the fact that he's treating them like royalty. In fact, whatever you do, don't-you-mention-them. You know how white folk is. They stick together. All you have to do is tell that man that I'm fed up. And if he don't do something, my girls and me are gonna be moving out, but this time for good!"

By now my father's head is in a quandary and he don't know what to think. Was she planning on killing two birds with one stone? Was this lengthy declaration aimed at him, as well? He'd never imagined she'd be thinking in such an intricate way. And was it possible she was thinking of going off and leaving him to look after the male children all by himself?

So, "That," exclaimed my father, "is the lousiest idea I've ever heard! And all it's going to do is make Mr. Miles angry and you know how mean he can be."

"Aw c'mon," snapped Mom. "So what do we have to lose honey? I'm willing to bet he don't want to lose a couple

175

of idiots like us. Think about it ... He didn't have to give us a dime for working forty acres. But he gave that white trash down there over $3,000 for working a mere twenty-five! Now it don't take no genius to figure that out. There ain't nobody in their right mind who'd pass up a couple of chumps like us."

"Now, that's just a matter of opinion," said my father. "We both know things ain't always the way they appear to be. That junk you're talking may sound good but that don't make it right."

"Why, Edmond," said Mama, as if talking to a child that just does not get it. "Please," she begged. "Give it some thought, honey. If we were in his shoes, we couldn't go wrong. But as long as we allow him to bounce us around, we'll be bouncing from now on. Can't you at least understand that much?"

Every word she said was true which she was sure of, so sure in fact, until she was comfortable enough to use them, to ridicule my father with.

"And one more thing," she said. "He's been taking advantage of you for a l-o-n-g time now, baby, which you cannot deny. And let's face it honey, he really got you last year, didn't he? Got you R-E-A-L good, now didn't he? Made you pay big time for moving out in the middle of the night. And you really screwed up when you asked him to sign for another of them 'ole used automobiles. Now need I say more?"

CHAPTER 43 "PRIVATE THOUGHTS"

My father didn't appreciate her adding scorn to his already volatile predicament, and especially since she had no idea of what he'd been thinking. He'd occasionally entertained the thought of escaping the cotton patch himself but these were private thoughts, which he hadn't garnered the courage to share with anyone. And since sharecropping was all he actually knew, he figured she'd probably frown upon his lofty dreams. He had eleven hungry mouths to feed, which didn't include he and my mom.

He also couldn't think of a time when he hadn't raised cotton or his own garden, and his hogs or borrowed from the country store. And he'd often asked himself, 'What would I do without Mr. Miles to look out for me?' And even occasionally asked, 'What would poor 'ole Mr. Miles do without me?' It was questions like these that kept him perpetually procrastinating. But thanks to my mom's aspirations, he'd finally gathered the courage to put up a decent fight...though he actually had no choice since she'd ignited such a fierce fire beneath him.

"If only," he said staring into the distance, "I could come out on top, just once. I'd move on up out of here so fast it'd make your head spin. And wouldn't even so much as look back!"

Since she'd never heard him speak in such a manner, Mom was actually taken by surprise! Yet she loved it - and even loved his choice of words.

So with an enthusiastic desire to egg him on, "That's it," she said! "Now you're talking," giving my father the confidence he needed. "That's it, baby," she said. "So just keep on talking!"

So with an optimistic gleam, my father straightened up and said with a positive burst of energy, "We could go someplace else and maybe even get a brand new start!"

"Now you sound like the man I married," said Mom.

"These folks don't care about us!"

"Ya' got that right," said Mom.

"They don't actually give a damn about none of us."

"You can say it again," shouted Mom!

"They work us from sun up,"

"C'mon now!"

"Work us till sun down!

"That's right!

"And if you get up on your feet,"

"Alright now,"

"Knock you right back down."

"C'mon wit' it!" "

"Knock you down to your knees!"

178

"Watch out now!"

"S-T-A-B you in your back!"

"Yes they will!"

"All the time they're riding around,"

"Unh Hunh!"

"in their brand new Cadillacs!"

"Well, Well," said Mom!

"The more you give,"

"I hear 'ya!"

"The more they'll take!"

"They'll take it!"

"And O-H-oh-oh, Lawd,"

"Come on now!"

"Rob you of your dignity!"

"YES they will!"

"Give you no respect!"

"Heard that!"

"Take everything you got and even hang you by your neck."

"Lord, ain't it the truth!"

179

"But O-O-O-O-H LORD," my father squalled.

"Now you're preaching Honey!"

"O-O-O-H LORD," repeated my father.

"Come on"

"I'm a-getting mighty tired!"

"Talk to me!"

"So- oo - oo tired!"

"So whatja gonna do?"

"I'ma Get up in the morning!"

"Yes Lord!"

"Stand up on my feet aha!"

"Watch out now!" "

"Hold my head up towards the sky!"

"Ahaunh!"

"Spread my wings and fly!"

"Come on with it!"

"Like a bird up in the sky!"

"Watch out now!"

"Oh! Oh! And one more thing I'm gonna do!"

180

"Talk to me now!"

"Ask the Good Lord to see me through!"

"Now you're preaching," said mother! "Now you're preaching!"

My father settled down and calmed his voice and he went back to work, yet in a more serious tone said, "This might surprise you, but I've been thinking of doing something different for a long time now. But since all I know is cotton, I don't know what that would actually be?"

Which was quite a shock as well, as far as mom was concerned.

"But this past year has really been an eye opener," said my dad. "Besides, I'm tired of this old man making a fool out of me."

"Well," said my mother, "once we break this yoke around our necks we ought to be able to figure something out. We've been hovering under his spell too long now."

"Instead of rushing off, I oughta be learning something new," said my father.

"From my point of view, we'll never gain the fortitude to escape if we don't do something pretty quick."

"I know," said Dad. "Whatever we decide to do, it has to be quick. But, on second thought, this might not be the way to do it."

"So what," insisted Mom, "do we have to lose? The way I see it, we have practically everything to gain. If you ask me, that old bastard could use a swift kick in the butt, especially after all he done-done to us. And I'm willing to bet the dog's got a guilt-

complex.

My dad didn't say another word. He simply scratched his head and went back to work. Mom started humming this old familiar tune, which my father immediately recognized and joined in with her. Their voices drifted through the trees and over fields and streams, and through meadows and throughout distant dells and valleys. *"Amazing Grace,"* they sang,

"How sweet the sound / That saved a wretch like me / I once was lost / But now I'm found / Was blind but now I see / was blind but now I see."

CHAPTER 44   "UNCLE JOE THE BABY MAKER"

Now my father's curly-headed, high-yellow, womanizing brother Joseph's wife was a mild mannered lady named Margie. And her husband was a rabble-rouser. But she, being barren of children, was as sweet as they come. And while most blacks bent their backs in the cotton patch, Uncle Joe rode around in his light blue Dodge Sedan making out with all of the available ladies. Yet, since she seemed to be happy just to be his wife, no one ever heard Aunt Margie complain.

Joseph was a nocturnal hunter who dawned himself with a battery-powered hat. And with the aid of his rifle and his bird dogs, he raised havoc on the creatures of the night. Unlike my father, he hunted for the sport of it and gave his catch to whomever he thought would appreciate it. And according to rumors, he sired up to thirty some-odd children, with at least half that many ladies. Yet my Aunt remained available to babysit those as well as other people's children. And being that he was rarely home, she worked the small plot they occupied on Joe Adam's plantation. It was she who became a part of my parents' plot by keeping the female children while my mother was away. My father meanwhile made arrangements with my grandmother in Clarksdale to keep the remaining boys.

So, two days after Thanksgiving, we all escorted Mom to the train station where my father's heart sank into the floor as the train pulled off.

He was supposed to play his part in a childless environment and was not suppose to mention the children. My parents had been together twenty some-odd years now and, in all that time, spent only several days apart, which my mom spent at her mother's house less than a mile away. So the fact that she'd be spending three weeks in California over 3000 miles away was quite a frightening situation.

And since the general rule among field hands forced into post-slavery servitude was excessive drinking and ramped-up confusion, no one appreciated sun up to sun down drudgery free of charge. A large, hard-working family with a non-drinking father figure was the average sharecropper's dream, come true. So, my parents' ability to stick together was the reason Mr. Miles was so fond of us.

And since his success depended on his talent to select stable field hands, no one appreciated this more than a seasoned cotton baron such as Edward Miles. And though he'd driven more than his share of good men to drink, he'd never knowingly embraced a drinking sharecropper. And this was the most coveted secret of his success.

CHAPTER 45   "CALIFORNIA"

Planning to question my dad and determine how deep to twist his screws into his obedient throat, the rotten-toothed scoundrel showed up at settlement time. After a quick study of my father's features, however, he decided to make light of the situation.

So, "Looks like," he said, "someone got a hold of you with an ugly stick and beat the pure D shit out of you!"

But instead of the response he expected, my father simply stood there with a sad look on his face.

"So what's wrong with you anyhow," he asked?

But my father simply stood there.

"Boy," repeated Mr. Miles, "did I ask you a question or what? I said what in the hell is wrong with you?"

"I'm afraid to say so," said my father.

"And exactly what does you mean?"

"Sorry sir", said my daddy, "but I'd rather not say!" Then as if he was trying to avoid the subject, "So how are you today," asked my father?

"Cut the shit, boy, and answer me!"

"Sorry," said Dad, "but I'm having a pretty rough day, sir."

"Ok," said Mr. Miles, "so what's that all about?"

"It's my wife, sir."

"Your wife! So what about her?"

"She's gone sir."

"Gone!!?"

"Yes sir, gone."

This was the last thing the old man wanted to or expected to hear.

"Gone where, boy?"

"Just gone, sir."

"But where, boy? You'd have to be out of your mind to let a gal like Magnolia get away. So what have you done to her anyhow? Is you playing with me, boy?"

"The Good Lord knows," said my father, "I wish I was, especially right along in here, sir, but it's not my fault."

"Well, now don't you worry," said Mr. Miles. "They always come back, don't they?"

"I know, sir. But I don't know about this time, sir. Maybe not," said Dad.

"I wouldn't worry about it," said the old man. "She couldn't be too far - probably hiding out at one of her sister's just a-waiting for you to come a-crawling on all fours. So now whata' you think?"

"Sure wish it was that simple," my daddy said, "but things ain't so simple, you know."

Suddenly the old man got angry and spat a wad of tobacco directly next to my father's foot. Yet, within his slicing gaze was a slight hint of fear.

'Well I'll be doggone,' he thought, 'Magnolia just might be right after all.'

Again Miles scanned the property and asked, "Did she take any of them chullen with her?"

But knowing it would penetrate, my father said, "Now, you know how she is about them girls, sir" - a vague answer which he purposefully left hanging in mid-air.

"Now just a minute," exclaimed the old man! "You've been a good God-fearing Christian practically ever since I've known you, boy, and a damn good field hand for twenty some-odd years. So now you ain't, went to drinking is you?"

"Oh, no sir," said my father. "You know I don't go out for that kind of stuff, sir."

"Well then I think, it's high time you tell me what you done-done to Magnolia!"

"Nothing," said my dad.

"Well, then why do you think she done run off and left your sorry ass? Though from the looks of ya', I can't say I blame her. So where do you think she done went to anyhow?"

That's when my father said, with the utmost pleasure, "Out to California, sir. I think they call it Los Angulus."

"Lost what?! What do you mean? Cali what?"

"California, sir."

"What in tarnation is you talking 'bout?"

"California, sir."

"Cali WHAT? But how?"

"On a train, sir."

"On a train! All the way out to California with an entire host of pickaninies? Why, that's pathetic, boy. What kind of a joke is this? This is some kind of a joke, ain't it? You is joking, ain't you? This is some sort of a cock-eyed joke? Ahh ha-ha-ha-ha!"

He then scanned the property as if expecting Mom and the rest of us children to come a-popping up out of nowhere. Then, "Alright," he said. "Stop your playing around, boy, and tell me what's up here? Is you clowning with me or what?"

"I wish I was," said Dad. "God knows how I do, and especially right along in here. But that's where Inez and Richard ran off to, and I hear they're pretty well established out there now - sunt tickets and everything."

"In that case, looks like you've got a problem," threatened Mr. Miles, "and I mean a damn big one, too!

Boy, you couldn't locate your own asshole without the aid of a white man I have to do everything except fart for your silly ass lately. So, What's that address?"

But what he doesn't know is my dad is tired, as well - of being talked down to, and referred to as 'boy' at the age of 49, and treated as if he was some sort of a farm animal. So he took his time and he stretched his words and waited as long as possible before saying, "I'm so sorry, but she didn't leave one."

"SHE DIDN'T WHAT," asked the old man?!

"Didn't leave one, sir. And frankly, I plum forgot to ask for one."

"Well now, then how is anyone supposed to get in touch with her? Boy, you must be out of your mind to allow your wife go so far out on a limb without so much as a digit for an address! So what kind of a fool is you?"

"You know Mr. Miles" said Dad? "That's something I've been thinking about."

"Well, you'd better get busy - and I mean pretty goddamn quick, too. And I'm giving you a week to - ten days the most."

"She promised to write," said my Dad, "before she left. And when she does she'll send me the address."

"So what's her complaint anyhow?"

"She's just tired, sir, plain ole' tired."

"Tired of what?"

"Of practically everything, sir - of breaking her back, day-in and day-out, and constantly being overworked and underpaid...tired of her children being denied an education. She's just tired sir, just plain ole' tired."

By now the old man is wishing he'd never questioned my father, but my father's on a roll.

"Tired of wearing raggedy clothes and shoes with holes in them, and tired of constantly being in the hole, sir. She just wants to live for a change, sir. And so does I sir, and so does I!" He also wanted to say 'we're tired of your old wrinkled ass, too,' but he knew better. The old man cut him short anyway.

"Now just a cotton-picking minute," he said! "Whoa, boy! Whoa-whoa! Now just a goddamn minute! Now I know what you been thinking, boy. I bet you anything I know what you've been thinking. You and Magnolia, y'all think y'all some smart ass nigras down here, don't you!? But you're wrong this time, boy. You got it all wrong, you hear? You got it all wrong this time! Y'all got the whole thing wrong! Things ain't always the way they appear to be, know what I mean? Now I'm telling you, y'all is got it all wrong."

Startled by the sudden shift of emotions, my father was struggling to keep up. Yet he clearly detected a new wave of fear in the old man's shaky throat. But not being sure of where he was coming from, he simply held his tongue.

190

"Now you know what a lease is, don't you boy, a lease? You know what a lease is, don't you? I said a lease, boy! You know what a lease is?"

"I suppose so," said my father, his mouth wide open.

"Well," said the old man pointing towards our white neighbor's property. "I leased that property to that fellow over there. He's a businessman just like me. Yeah, that's right, he's a businessman. He's in business for his self, just like me. You understand? Yeah that's right, you understand?"

He's lying through his teeth. And even if he wasn't, our family was getting a royal screwing. Cause' if twenty-five acres could produce that much revenue then forty should've produced practically twice as much. My father was at least that astute. The forty acres we worked were also leased at a cost of $12.50 an acre. But thanks to my mother's initiative, my dad was finally in the position to perform a settlement of his own. So he asked a question, which he'd never had the courage to pursue.

"So, what," he asked, "about that $400 you added to my account which you claim you paid Mr. Crawford on our behalf," which caused the old man to sputter and spit tobacco juice all over the place. Yet he admonished my father with a threat.

"You wouldn't be worth a two-shaded piece of dog shit without Magnolia," he shouted! And immediately before dusting him with his rear wheels, "I'm giving you a week to ten days," he said. "And if Magnolia ain't back by then, I want your black ass off my property!"

191

192

CHAPTER 46   "BACK HOME AGAIN"

Well, as God would have it, Mom would never be happy under her previous circumstances. She'd seen life from a different perspective and when she returned, she had California at the brain. Mom actually wanted to share her adventure with Dad but he was much too busy trying to make the best of his mundane situation. Yet he was all puffed up about the way he handled the situation with Mr. Miles who extended himself in an unusual manner. About a week prior to Christmas, he showed up with gifts for the entire family: gave my mother a receipt for a brand new wood burning stove and my father a fancy looking pocket watch. And he brought a crate of apples and one of oranges for the entire family to enjoy. My parents didn't quite know how to deal with such a sudden windfall, and my father must've thanked the man a thousand times.

He then invited my father into his car, which he referred to as his office, for a chat. And they sat there in his Ford Coupe for a while. But once he emerged and stepped back inside, Mom asked had Mr. Miles mentioned the $400, which he hadn't.

So gazing at him through suspicious eyes, she said, "You sold your entire family out for a crate of apples and oranges didn't you?"

"But," my father said cutting his eyes across the room, "why are you being so hard on the man? Why don't you give him credit for what he done-done already?"

"It's not him I'm worried about," said Mom. "It's you, Edmond - that's who I'm worried about."

"Aw c'mon," said my father. "You just done went out there to California and got your head all filled up with foolishness."

"Foolishness," she repeated? "I'll show you some foolishness, if that's what you wanta' to see. I'll show you some foolishness, alright. Now the last thing my daughter said before I left there was any time I was ready, all I had to do was call her and she'll send me tickets for the rest of my girls and me. Now that's me, and the rest of my girls! So I'm not about to put up with your foolishness, nor old man Miles' too much longer. So get that through that thick skull of yours. Because I've just about had it with both of you!"

My father wasn't used to her talking like this. It was much too unusual. He'd always known our half sister Inez hated his guts and would do anything to break them up - a progression he suspected might already be in place - so the argument escalated. Yet mom ended up informing him that if he didn't start finding a way out of their current situation, she and her female children were going to pack up and leave.

The following year, Mr. Miles took an extra $160 from them at settlement time, part of which was for the last car my father purchased. But adding fuel to the fire, he told them the white family was about to move on, and propositioned my parents and the family on the opposite side of them to split their plot up between them. This was the straw that broke the camel's back. For both my parents agreed that the time had come to finally get out of The Triple B System.

194

BBB
SYSTEM

CHAPTER 47 "MOVING ON UP AND OUT"

So, once again, the family was prepared to move under the cover of night. But Mom's Uncle Tom stepfather was hanging around keeping an eye out for Mr. Miles, so we dared not pack until the night of the move. It was no secret that Mr. Miles had him looking out for him but we were family and even we couldn't trust the old broken down fool.

Dad borrowed a trailer from my uncle Ernest who lived two miles south of Clarksdale and who worked on a more progressive level of the cotton chain. He walked around in creased khaki pants and was respected by his peers. The men he worked for were much more progressive than Mr. Miles could've ever hoped to be.

The Hopkins brothers had at least ten times the land Mr. Miles possessed and they functioned on a much higher level. My uncle was the Hopkins brother's straw boss - a Negro who keeps other Negros in line for their white overseers. It was he who introduced my father to a man looking for a large family to work a plot just above Clarksdale. My dad figured should he get that close to town, he'd possibly learn another trade and maybe even get out of the cotton business for good, though he had no idea what that would be. Yet he figured practically anything would beat his current condition.

The owner of the plot showed my parents the place amid a frozen winter's night in the wake of a severe snowstorm. And as desperate as they were, had they viewed the property in the summertime and during

196

daylight hours, they would've certainly passed on the deal. Though the house did have the first flushable toilet they'd ever experienced, running water and an electric light, there was still much to be desired. In fact, had either of them known it was once a funeral parlor, the deal would have been automatically null and void!

The house sat on a knoll with a panoramic view from its rear window. And merely twenty feet beyond the front door was a black top road. It ran between the house and the railroad tracks where, in due time, they'd come to realize was quite a busy artery from dusk to dawn. An eighty foot smoke stack, which harbored its secrets, was situated about a hundred yards behind the house. They'd seen the thing but only against the night sky...and its shape was just about all they could discern.

Since the owner always claimed to be too busy to show it during daylight hours, my parents didn't really know the finer details of the situation. He was such a shrewd operator who knew how to play a prospective tenant. For once he took them inside, and turned that electric light on which, for someone who'd never experienced such a thing, was a futuristic experience. From that moment on, there was no way to determine the outer perimeters of the property.

He'd also convinced my parents that, since the house was on a hilly terrain, he'd rather them not walk down at the base of the property for fear they might slip and fall, which he said as if he was truly looking out for their interest. They'd made up their minds not to work for Mr. Miles another day, so they figured this opportunity -

197

which my father's brother-in-law had introduced them to - was quite a blessing. And since - other than Mr. Crawford's renewed offer - this was the only remaining opportunity, they decided to move...in spite of all.

My mom and dad, James Lee and Grady and Jessie Mae worked through the night. They started loading the trailer at 10:30PM. But just before it was fully loaded, Dad's brother-in-law showed up in a huge, red International truck, which they used to transport field hands. My mother and father regarded this as a blessing. And, 'oh what a blessing,' they thought! But in fact, it was their new boss' insurance policy, for he'd paid my uncle and gave him money for his two hired helpers who came along with him.

Edna Rea, Frankie D, all the younger children and myself practically slept through the ordeal and had no idea what was going on. My mom and dad wanted to make sure no leaks got out, and especially where her stepfather was concerned. Edward Miles, they figured, was meaner than the devil himself. But he was a cloak-less adversary. My mother's stepfather, on the other hand, was lower than a snake in the grass. If it weren't for their love of our grandmother, they would've long since excommunicated the old broken down fool. For it is traitors, such as he that were, and who will always be, among the lowest of the low.

CHAPTER 48 "THE PIG PEN ON SCAVENGER'S ROW"

A southern-bound freight split the morning silence into bits and pieces as it came crashing into the southern atmosphere. Just like that, it came from out of nowhere - a humongous thing so powerful it made the earth quiver. Metal clanged and clacked as nails in the turn-of-the-century house shrieked against the dawn. Shock waves rippled throughout the hearts and minds of every individual, none whom in our wildest nightmares could've ever imagined such a thing. The rumbling lingered on and on...and eventually, it faded into an eerie, disheartening silence.

The pungent aroma of burnt coal fell from the sky, and drifted into the cracks and crevices, adding yet another layer of bewilderment to our already confused awakenings. In the immediate wake of the confusion, everyone was wide awake and up and on their feet struggling to figure out what had just taken place.

Suddenly, yet *another* mile long freight came a running in the opposite direction, blowing its boisterous whistle as it let off steam and shook the earth to its very core! Then, slightly after 8:00AM, a parade of orange colored trucks lined up outside of Clarksdale and dominated the blacktop, which ran between the railroad tracks and the house. Each of these turned some hundred yards beyond the shack and onto a gravel road which they traveled another hundred feet or so. Then turned directly into the Clarksdale City Dump. The grotesque view from my parents' bedroom window was enough to make a billionaire feel like an out and out failure.

There it was - a huge unbelievable thing - all laid out across the vastness of the landscape. My parents had seen the smokestack but as a mere backdrop in the darkened sky and assumed since it was so close to town, it had something to do with commerce. Neither imagined that it was an overblown contraption where the city cremated everything from a mouse to a full-grown horse. Nor that the stench of both burnt animal hair and flesh, would cast such a foul odor while spreading its vectoring fumes across the sky. Yet it and the city dump were not the only drawbacks, for shortly after 8:00 A.M., a pair of bulldozers started manipulating the filth which caused the effect of the dump to become even more apparent.

None of these compared to the owner's son's pigpen, though. The gates of Hell themselves couldn't have held a twig to such a maggot-infested site.

The boy's family owned the largest, independent grocery store in Clarksdale. And they also had a hog pen opposite the lopsided shack next to ours, which sat directly up on the rotten contrivance. There, the son raised some of the healthiest looking hogs in the state. The boy fed them Corn Flakes, Rice Crispies, Wheat Puffs and practically every kind of cold cereal gone bad. Nestle Crunch, Babe Ruth, Payday, Powerhouse and Mars candy bars by the wormy carton full. His family also owned the largest fish market in Clarksdale. And on a scale of one to ten, a rotten fish head had to rate at

200

least a twelve. The boy dumped them into the pig's pen by the tubful, which caused such an overwhelming volume of stench until the dump, in comparison, could've been a mild deodorant bar. The hogs waded through it all, trampling it into a muddy mixture of cold cereal, rotten vegetables, worm infested candy bars, fish heads and hog shit!

So during the summertime, each and every breath was reduced to a painful experience. The wintertime had a subtle funk of its, own. But even that, depending on the wind's direction, was just as devastating. My parents were in now and couldn't move without losing their honor. Yet to remain was an honor unto the devil himself.

It was the extreme bottom of the pits for me whose tenth birthday was approaching. I hated everything except the activity on the railroad, which was the main line in the Upper Mississippi Delta, and was the only equitable aspect of the situation.

Frankie D. and me, in our desperate attempt to maintain our sanity, entered into an affectionate relationship with steam engines. We both fell head over heels in love with the huge, smoky things, many of which stopped in front of our house either to refuel or water up. Such a thrill it was to wave at the train's crew and engineers who wore grey striped overalls with caps that matched. Whenever one waved back, our hearts exploded with joy.

Less than a hundred yards beyond our house opposite the entrance to the dump, there was a huge wooden water tower where at least 30% of the trains stopped. Some stopped for water while others stopped for fuel. Then there were those that stopped to pick up boxcars on a switched track.

The activity on the railroad added a new dimension to our lives, so the two of us all of sudden began to see life in a different light. We'd seen trains before but usually from a distance and strictly by chance. But to see them up-close and so often was quite a thrill. Oft times, trains didn't stop to refuel but stuck around switching boxcars and tankers - some of which they took and others of which they left. Frankie D. and I studied the contraptions, which in our minds were bigger than life itself! They'd often huff and puff, spin their huge wheels, blow their whistles... going no place at all. Others passed at the speed of greased lightening leaving us with a spinning-in-the-head sensation.

Our favorite was a huge smoky engine with big white numbers that read #1136. It was the boldest, fastest, huffing-and-puffing thing you could ever imagine! She was both the classiest and swiftest steam engine in all of God's creation. She'd oft-times stop to drink. And when she did, we'd watch her with wide-eyed amazement, all the while wishing she'd never leave, and all the time yearning to get closer - close enough to touch - but we knew we never would. Her engineers appeared to be so proud. One would be inside turning knobs and pulling all sorts of levers, while the other climbed the curved ladder and stood atop the majestic engine. He then grabbed the rope dangling from the funnel and ran gallons upon gallons of water into her huge black belly, then walk back to the coal chute where he'd fill her bin with coal. Then, as soon as they'd finished, she'd let out a billow of steam, whistle several times, and take off like a bat out of Hell!

And as she diminished in size, we'd feel an emptiness coming over us. We knew she was going places far beyond our imagination.

Being that I was 10 and Frankie D. was 8, it'd taken us eighteen years to travel only eleven miles from where we were born. #1136 did this in ten minutes time and at least 600 times a day. And were either of us elected to participate in a contest as to which was the greatest locomotive of all-time, #1136 would've won hands down!

CHAPTER 49 "A MOST DIFFICULT SITUATION"

My dad's new boss was a shrewd son of a gun. He knew exactly how to play his cards. So it was an entire month before he'd show his face again.

My dad was traumatized by then and had all but lost his sense of smell. Mr. Merritt, on the other hand, was a sharecropper-come-city-slicker-pimp who'd played this particular scenario time and time again.

Finally, the huge-headed, red-faced charlatan with a nervous system equivalent to an arctic icicle resurfaced. He sat his sun burnt elbow in the window of his Chrysler Sedan then cocked his heavy head aside, looked my daddy directly in the eyes and asked, "So, how do you like it, Sambo?" But before he chanced to answer, "Boy," said Mr. Merritt, "the view from the top of a hill sure makes you feel kind of special, don't it?"

Dumbfounded, my daddy wondered if he truly thought anyone could appreciate such a wretched predicament. His first inclination was to tell the shyster what he was actually thinking. But on second thought, he was under a three-year contract, which he was hoping to get out from under in a timely manner. He, therefore, decided to play it cool.

And though it went against every grain of his conviction he finally heard himself saying, "Well, it's alright sir but-"

But the charlatan cut him off again.

"By the way," he said, "you've got a great deal here, though I realize how my boy's pig pen can be kind of a nuisance. But look at it like this: at least you don't have to put up with it first-hand like that old couple over there! Ha, ha, ha, ha, ha," he chuckled while nodding toward the rickety shack between our house and the pig's pen. Then he motioned towards the dump. "You'll get used to all this in time, boy. In fact, you won't even know it exists after awhile - and especially when the sun goes down. You'll be so busy during cotton season, you won't even hardly know it exists."

"But Mr. Merritt," said my dad. "This is the most difficult situation I've ever been in, sir. I was hoping you had someplace that wasn't surrounded by so much confusion, sir."

"Surrounded by confusion," repeated Merritt, his face suddenly redder than a beet? "Listen," shouted Merritt above the noisy bulldozers! "Boy, I'd taken a liking to you which is the reason I gave you this particular spot. It's one of the best spots I've got. Now I done told you from the beginning there were at least a dozen other nigras and several white families begging to gain access to this property. Yet just because I favored your black ass, I gave it to you!"

My dad tried to get a word in edgewise but...

"That's precisely what I say about your people. Give them an inch and they'll take a mile every fucking TIME! And I mean every mother-fucking time! So, how many

205

nigras do you know with running water and electric lights and a flushable toilet? It's like I said: give you an inch and you'll take a mile every time."

"But I don't..." exclaimed my daddy.

"Hell, you ought to be thanking me from the bottom of your ungrateful heart! That's what you ought to be doing!"

"I do appreciate your generosity, Mr. Merritt. But this," my daddy said, "is the most difficult situation I done ever been in!"

"Well a bargain is a bargain," he said. "And you and me, we made a bargain."

"But can't we at least discuss this," said my father?

"Hell naw! We ain't got a damn thing to discuss, boy! Like I said, a bargain is a bargain! Now I don't want to hear another goddamn word, you hear," he said before slamming his foot to the floor.

Another orange colored truck came from the opposite direction. And as it turned into the dump, a gunnysack fell from its tailgate and splattered filth across the roadway. A monstrous freight, at the same time, came a crashing into the scene, drowning out everything - the noisy bulldozers included! So, in an attempt to override the chaos, my dad covered his ears and rushed back inside where the confusion, though it continued, was not so apparent anymore.

206

CHAPTER 50   "A NASTY RUMOR"

The only advantage we had on Merritt's plantation was one of cultivation because he did something Mr. Miles would've never considered. He sent a tractor in early spring to turn the land under which my father always did with the aid of a single blade plow and his mule team. That took several weeks to a month to complete, yet the tractor did the same job within a day-and-a-half, then he sent the tractor back in late spring. So, for the first time in his career, my father had no use for mules.

The electricity consisted of only a single light bulb, which hung in the center of the living room. The toilet was the first flushable one we'd seen but it, too, was attached to the outside of the house. We, therefore, had to go outside to use it, but it rarely flushed properly. And beyond that it had the most humongous cockroaches I'd ever seen!

My uncle told my dad he was required to have his own car when he first mentioned this supposed opportunity. Especially since the greater part of the cotton patch was on the outer surrounding of the dump. The closest section was less than a quarter of a mile from the house. We, therefore, picked from the furthest distance then worked our way back towards the house. So by the time we finished, the season would be over and that was usually around Thanksgiving.

In that year they introduced Dorothy Jean, who was the next youngest child, to the cotton patch, so our four year-old baby brother George had to also come along.

Both Mom and Dad took turns pulling him on their sacks and, as usual, we were up at sunrise. But instead of walking, we all piled into the car, at least some of us did until someone could double back to pick the rest up. The situation with Frankie D. and me was reversed now because we preferred the cotton patch to being at home. The stench surrounding the house was so strong it could destroy a mad dog's appetite, and was so overwhelming until we rarely enjoyed a decent meal anymore.

The ground, which forced us to work harder than usual, was twice as tough as that we were used to, so we were so tired come nightfall until we could barely eat. We'd always had a garden but not here - for there was no place to plant one. Eventually, the entire family took on a grayish-like hue. My mom tried to plant a garden at the edge of the cotton patch but she had no way to water it. So they eventually came up with Plan B and sent me to work as a hired helper on one of my uncle's trucks.

I earned, as did each individual on the crew, seventy-five cents a day, which, believe it or not, was more than enough to make up for the garden. And since I was his relative and the youngest on the crew, my uncle assigned me the water boy position. As water boy, I didn't have to chop but anytime I wasn't dispensing water, I was obligated to carry a hoe, which was mostly for show in case his boss showed up.

One morning, my dad had something else to do so he dropped me off at the square where trucks picked up field hands and I sat there for the longest. Then, finally, people started coming out of the woodworks and soon there were enough to fill every truck in the square. A nasty rumor was going around that day which frightened the daylights out of most field hands. No one was sure but my uncle's truck was one of those, which fell under suspicion. I heard a field hand ask my uncle for his destination. But avoiding the man's eyes my uncle said, "Now you know good and well I'm not supposed to divulge that particular information, now don't you?"

CHAPTER 51 "A BUMPY RIDE WITH THE FAT LADY"

Most people preferred their own choice of straw boss if, for no other reason, the crew remained the same. So when the final count was in, everyone looked pretty much the same that day.

My uncle eased out on Highway 61 and headed north, then continued for at least a half an hour. He then turned onto a bumpy gravel road, which we bumped along on for what seemed like a lifetime. The heat was so intense now and some field hands were becoming restless. In fact, you could actually cut the tension with a knife. And then, all of a sudden, someone said, "This motherfucker's taking us to the forties!"

"What," asked another?!

"He's taking us to the forties!"

"You're kidding," said another!

An older gentleman stood up and said, "Something told me not to get on this motherfucker! So why didn't I follow my mind!"

"Lawd," said the fat lady who sat next to me. "We is in for it today, child. We is really, really in for it!"

I sat there dumbfounded and had no idea what they were talking about. I knew they had a place on Mr. Miles' plantation called 'the far twenties,' but the reason they called it that was because it was so far away from

210

the shack. So, at least in my mind, it didn't seem like anything to go getting all bent out of shape for.

The morning was cool when we started out but the temperature now had risen dramatically. So by the time we reached our destination, practically every field hand had a funky attitude. And a single look at the soil, revealed their initiative. For it was blacker than coal and, for all intents and purposes, harsher in appearance. The frail cotton was incrementally succumbing to Johnson grass and weeds.

Most all of them were complaining and for several legitimate reasons. No one in their right mind liked cutting into severe soil. Adding to our dilemma was the heat, and the Johnson grass, which grows taller and faster than all other grasses with razor sharp leaves that'll slash you to shreds before you even know you've been cut. Only after you've bled for a while does its vicious sting start and that's when you'll realize how injured you actually are. Its roots are tougher than all other grasses put together. So chopping Johnson grass isn't simply a chore, it's a defilement.

Now, being Straw Boss for a long time, my uncle was an expert at his craft. So he kept a sharp hoe in a particular place on his truck. The first thing he did was grab his hoe which he dug into the rigid soil and chopped about fifteen or twenty feet up one row and back on another. Meanwhile, those who'd denounced the affair concentrated on the zing of his hoe until, he finally, looked up and said, "Aw shucks, this ain't so bad. Hell, I thought it was gonna be worser than this!"

211

The fat lady who sat next to me rolled her eyes into the sky, indicating my uncle was full of shit, then lifted her hoe and headed for one of the pre-chopped rows. "We's out here," she said, "so we might as well do what we came out here to do." Then she lowered her hoe and dug into the petrified soil with it.

The rest of the crew eventually fell in line, yet, some were still complaining. But to conserve energy, their blabbering faded beneath the clamor of their hoes.

CHAPTER 52   "THE GREEN STUDEBAKER"

I grabbed a hoe and slashed into the brittle surface but the handle practically jarred my hands to bits. So my Uncle Tom, who simply walked around with a hoe on his shoulder, said, "Forget that son! Just go get the water bucket and pass it around."

The bucket was a three-gallon zinc apparatus with a dipper that matched and from which most people drank directly. Some brought their own utensils like the fat lady who had an accordion-like thing, which she'd pull open and drink from then squeeze it back together. The heat was so intense that I was still going back and forth from hand to mouth an hour-and-a half later. Some people wanted more before I could double back. And by the time the sun reached its apex, we were all feeling as though the forces of Hell were upon our backs.

Just before noon, my uncle - who'd long since devised ways of doing nothing - pulled his sluggish rump up from beneath a tree. He reached in his cab and got a bottle of whiskey, which he took a hearty swig of. Then went around to the side and secured the water barrel after which he blew his horn. And since the thought of resting their limbs was so overpowering, this was quite a welcoming signal.

So we bumped our way back up to the gravel road and headed, once again, towards Highway 61, then headed north an additional three-and-a-half miles. On the side of the road, there was a general store-come-service station where my uncle parked parallel to the highway. I was one of the first of the twenty some odd workers who got off. The remaining crew either brought their own lunches or asked others to bring them something. Some wanted cheese and crackers, others bologna and light bread, but most requested an RC, grape, orange or strawberry soda.

There were several medium-size fans blowing inside the store, which seemed to be buzzing like buzz saws. My uncle gave me a 25-cent advance of which I purchased two slices of bologna for 8 cents each, a 5-cent Pepsi-Cola and a bag of salted peanuts for yet another nickel. There were so many people in the store, all lined-up to pay for their merchandise. And this was the first time I'd been in a store with three cash registers, manned by three youthful looking white ladies. There were two other trucks of hungry field hands ahead of us so, needless to say, the ladies were earning their living.

But I had never heard anything like the noise I heard when I exited the store. So, focusing in the direction of the disturbance, I realized it was hot rubber grinding against asphalt. But what I saw next practically scared the daylights out of me.

It was the driver of a green Studebaker, gripping his steering wheel while leaning to the right and struggling to change an out of control situation - a double-chinned white fellow turning the wheel to the left as his car continued to skid in the opposite direction. Beads of sweat the size of BB's popped out on his forehead and he appeared to be gripping every nerve and muscle in his body! And judging from the look in his bulging eyes, fear and tension had all but captivated his heart, mind and soul. So with a bird's eye view on my uncle's truck, which he was rapidly closing in on, he seemed preoccupied with ridding himself of a Jack Daniels bottler, which he somehow managed to squeeze until it exploded. He then spotted the fat lady who, at a snail's pace, climbed the truck's ladder and immediately knew she was moving much too slow. Everything it seemed, even to a spectator such as I, was suddenly moving in slow motion. But then he spotted another field hand, a deaf mute who hadn't heard the noise and then another who looked him dead in the eye which was among the most horrifying looks either man would ever see - for they both saw death in its indisputable description, and knew they'd be the last to see one another alive.

In a last ditch effort, he applied both feet to the brakes but it was futile. So he swallowed the huge lump within his expanding throat and, "OH, SHIT! OH, MY GOD! LORD HAVE MERCY! JESUS CHRIST! OH, MY GOD! SHIT! OH!!!"

A BAMA LAMA LANG ALANG CHANG, CHANG ALAM A LANG, LANG!

There's blood and dust everywhere. The Studebaker is all crunched up in front and is bouncing backwards in mid-air. There's pain and dust and total confusion everywhere, and the driver appears to be either dead or severely wounded. And there lays the fat lady, bleeding profusely between the Studebaker and the back of the truck, at least what's left of her wrangled body. Her

215

spirit, however, is fleeing ever so swiftly into a future existence.

The last fellow who looked the driver in the eyes is dead as well, his body like that of the deaf mute's, practically crushed beyond recognition. There are others on the truck bleeding from the mouths and nostrils, and their heads are filled with confusion - some with blood streaming down their foreheads and others who are simply dazed or knocked unconscious.

There were a few injured whites, too, though none quite so directly hit. None of their injuries was life threatening, except the driver of the Studebaker, whose lap was playing host to the car's engine and whose chest, was crushed by its steering column. Almost immediately, though, there was ambulance service for the whites. It seemed they came out of nowhere! And, of course, their operators were much too grand to touch a wounded black. They had to wait for the hearses from Clarksdale's black funeral homes 30 some-odd miles away. By the time they arrived, however, more people had died. Others waited until the hearses could return to pick them up.

I stood at the roadside crying for the wounded and for the dead. My uncle eased up behind me and said, "It's o.k. to cry, son. But don't forget to be thankful you weren't on that truck when this happened. What would I have told your parents?"

And though he was trying to hide it, he, too, was on the verge of tears.

216

CHAPTER 53 "OF MULATTOS, FRIENDS AND HALF BROTHERS"

Less than 150 yards on the opposite side of the railroad tracks was the sketchy outskirts of Clarksdale where F & H Food Market sat on a corner to itself. The proprietor and his wife ran the store on the weekends but, on weekdays, left it in charge of their two teenage sons: a mulatto named Eddie and a younger brother Jimmy who also helped around the store. Jimmy, the youngest son, lived a lonely existence and had few friends, if any, before Frankie D. and I came along. So anytime he saw us coming, he'd light up like a Christmas tree! He was older than us, but in the void of loneliness, age often loses its measure, so we'd been playing with the chubby little sucker for a while. And accepted him as a friend.

Yet when we arrived at the store on his 14th birthday, Jimmy was standing in his usual spot with his chest expanded. I spoke to the boy who was always overjoyed to see us, but he refused to speak. In fact, he acted as if he didn't recognize either of us. So I spoke again.

But this time, he asked in the rudest manner, "What's that you say, nigger?"

Now this was not the first time I experienced the dilemma, which I'd experienced under slightly different circumstances. But had no antidote for the attitude. So I immediately opened the door and went directly into the store. And though he was forced to breathe harder, Jimmy walked swiftly behind us and rudely shouted,

217

"Nigger, what'd I say?"

"I just said hi, Jimmy, that's all."

"Well now, is that the way to address a white man," he asked? "I want both of you jiggaboos to understand something. I'm a man now, a full-grown man. I turned fourteen today and I think it's high time I get some fucking respect around here!"

Frankie D. and I stood there, our mouths and eyes wide open while Jimmy's older brothers were pretending - at least according to their expressions - that they were just as surprised as we were. But I could tell Jimmy was showing off for the sake of the older boys, though I had rushed into the doorway hoping he'd be ashamed to pursue his rude attack in their presence, and certainly not in the presence of mulatto! The mulatto, whom I suspected was a half brother to the rest, had always played tickling games with Frankie D. and me whenever we came into the store.

Yet it didn't take long to realize the older boys had put him up to this. So attempting to avoid what I knew was coming, I started rapping off items from my mother's list. But the boy over rode me.

"And another thing," he said, "I want you jiggaboos to understand. From now on," he said, "y'all say yassir and naw sah to me. And don't neither one of you black sons of bitches twist your liver lips to say 'yes' and 'no' again, you hear? Is that clear? Goddamn it, I said is it fucking clear?!"

218

He was looking directly down Frankie D's throat as he spewed his rude instructions.

Frankie D. bucked his eyes and shuddered then said, "Yes... ah-ah, I mean yassir."

The boy then looked up at his older brothers, one of which smiled and gave a nod of approval.

Meanwhile, I looked at all of them, including the black fool who acted as if he was as proud of Jimmy as his white half brothers. And even though his eyes were green and his skin was lighter, he actually appeared more akin to us than he did them. But one would be hard pressed to convince him of that.

He then swung me around by the elbow.

"NIGGER," he shouted, "don't you dare ignore me when I'm talking! From now on, whenever I speak, I expect your undivided attention, you hear?! I'm a full-grown man now - a white man - which means I have full authority to kick dead off into your black ass any time I so goddamn please! And I mean any goddamn time I so please, you hear?!"

So searching for the smallest trace of shame, I looked far beyond the boy's speckled pupils, yet saw nothing but an empty void. We'd befriended this little chubby clown for the better part of a year now. And Frankie D. and I had begun to think of him as an honest to goodness, genuine friend. So I searched deeper, searching for the slightest sign of guilt, but detected none - none whatsoever. So, 'Why,' I wondered, 'would anyone in his right mind exchange an affectionate little chubby

219

personality like the one we thought we knew for anything so vile and so unnecessarily evil?' But by that time, Jimmy was digging his index finger into my chest.

"Boy," he said. "I asked you if you understood what I was talking about!"

It took all I had to unleash my tongue. Yet, finally, I heard myself say, "Yassir, Mr. Jimmy. Yassir. I, I understand, sir. I truly do, sir. I understand."

"Well then, that's better, goddamn it," said the boy.

Then, breathing deeply, he turned and walked around the store like a conceited cock, his fat arms dangling swiftly from his shoulders, all the while scanning us as we stood there, our mouths and eyes wide open. He looked once again up at his older brothers, "High time," he said. "I get some fucking respect around here, SHIT!"

The affair had practically drained him of his energy. So looking quite exhausted, he went and sat in the corner of the store on an orange crate.

"Well now," said one of the older boys in a calmer tone, "now that we've got that settled, why don't we get on down to business? So what about this note: this grocery list of yours?"

And while the older boys gathered groceries, the mulatto tried to tickle Frankie D. and me again. Now one of the main reasons we'd always looked forward to coming to the store was to play with Jimmy. But we truly enjoyed being tickled by that mulatto, and always got a kick out of him pretending the slightest touch

220

anywhere on his cowardly body gave him an urge to jump completely out of his skin.

However, from that day forward, the very thought of him touching us served only to remind us that his heart was as empty and as shallow as the void in his younger brother's eyes. And on that particular day, we'd all lost something. The chubby boy lost two genuine friends while both Frankie D. and I lost respect for Jimmy and his older brothers. The mindless mulatto, however: was more than likely the biggest loser of us all.

CHAPTER 54 "UPSIDE DOWN AND INSIDE OUT"

My father made an inquiry about a vacant house in Clarksdale, and so he rushed home to tell my mother about it. We'd stayed in the dump long enough to satisfy Merritt's contract, so we were finally ready to make our move. My mom was pleased so my father went back and put a deposit on it.

When they first became associated with Mr. Merritt, he'd promised to fix it so Mr. Miles could never find our family again. Yet merely three days before the move, the old man showed up. My parents didn't know Mr. Miles smelled a rat long before they pulled out in the middle of the night, nor did they realize he'd been fantasizing about Mr. Jack Crawford hounding my father again. So he took the liberty to rearrange our fate.

Most importantly, my parents had no idea that both Mr. Merritt and Mr. Miles were first cousins, and they had come together for the purpose of laying a trap. So rearing back now in his new Ford Coupe, thinking he has my father exactly where he wants him, "Well," he asked? "Is you ready to come home and get on back down to business, boy?"

"Down to business," said my father taken totally by surprise?

"That's right boy, back down to business!"

"But, Mr. Miles," asked Dad. "What do you mean?"

"I mean business, or have you become too accustomed to this goddamn dump?"

Shocked, my father simply stood there.

"How many times I done told you, ain't a white man in this county who'll treat you as good as I do! Well, I'll be damned," added the shyster, "If it don't smell like ten pounds of frozen antelope ass out here! So how much of this shit can you take anyhow?"

In an effort to confirm the old man's inquiry, my father made a detailed assessment of the atmosphere but he couldn't smell, nothing. The stench, by now, he figured, had become as much a part of him as he had of it. And since he couldn't smell anything, he figured he, too, must've smelt as bad as both the pigpen and the dump put together.

Yet he resented the old man setting up stake in his yard, as if he'd come to collect a piece of personal property. So he reflected on their lengthy association, which he resented also resented since he couldn't think of but a single day when he wasn't mired in misery. But, oh, what a day that was! The old man, meanwhile, sat in his car slamming my father with the vilest language. But it didn't stop my father from reveling in the memory of that one special day. The day he took control of his own destiny. And though it lasted a few precious moments, it was one he'd never forget. That was THE day he went against the old man's will - the day he took his very dear old time to dawn himself with his hip boots.

'Now that was a day,' he repeated. 'When the old goat

223

got stuck in his pigpen, and was inundated with tons of hog shit, and he couldn't do a damn thing about it - when the entire family enjoyed a chuckle at the old tobacco chewing goat's expense. 'Now that,' he thought, 'was a day!'

From the very beginning, my daddy knew he was at a disadvantage and could not compete with the old man, who owned 400 acres of fertile land while he, himself didn't own a single inch. Yet he had the strength to work the land, which without he and his kind, the likes of Mr. Miles would cease to exist. It also dawned on him that there were elements he could relate to which would scare the shit out of Mr. Miles, who couldn't survive a single day in his shoes. So he cast his eyes across the dump once again of which he'd long since become a part of.

Meanwhile, the old man, spat virgin streams of tobacco down the side of the door of his brand new car.

"You're not the dumbest nigra I know, but you're about the sneakiest son of a bitch I've ever laid eyes on," he said in reference to my dad's escape in the middle of night. He might as well have said 'you can run but you just can't hide.'

My father once again cast his eyes across the dump, but this time he focused on the rotten fish heads. Knowing good and well he should smell the fish heads but they, too, escaped his ability to smell.

CHAPTER 55 "DOING SOMETHING DIFFERENT"

And though the tobacco juice spewing from the old man's mouth contained less, stench than the pig's pen, his tongue spared no mercy.

So after suffering blow after blow of the most degrading remarks, my father decided to at least clear his mind. And though he heard himself saying "I'm sorry," he most assertively added, "I don't think my family and me is gonna pick no more cotton, sir. And don't have the slightest intentions of coming back down there to work for you. Now I'm sorry sir but I been thinking of doing something different for a change."

To this the old man's mouth flew wide open and suddenly his face was cloudy.

"These old hands," my father said holding them out in front of him, "done picked enough cotton for a hundred men. So, you see sir, our time has come Mr. Miles and we was hoping to do this with your blessings."

But that phrase, 'doing something different', kept on reoccurring in the old man's mind. So he reached into his pocket and pulled out a fresh slab of chewing tobacco. He then bit into it as hard as possible with his rotten teeth. "Boy, you is really something," he said. "I mean you is really something. So what do you know how to do besides working in a cotton patch?"

225

A long moment of emptiness incurred as my father stumbled through a litany of worthless words in an effort to rationalize his position, yet he had no logical alternative.

"Let's face it," said the old man. "You're a natural born cotton-picker, which is about all you'll ever amount to. So why don't you just stick to what you know and leave the rest to me."

"But there's no doubt in my mind," said Dad, "that I want to do something different. Now that much I know. I may not know what that is yet, but I do know that much."

"Well I-mo tell ya what you gonna be doing," said Mr. Miles as he turned ten shades redder, "not a goddamn cock-sucking thing! That's what you gonna be doing. Not a goddamn cock-sucking thing! That's exactly what you're gonna be doing!"

"But, Mr. Miles sir, I'm just trying to do something to better my condition."

"You can finish medical school, go to barber-college and even get a law degree, but you *still* won't get so much as a sniffle on a job in this county, now that much I guarantee!"

"But, Mr. Miles," pleaded Dad, "it just don't seem fair."

"As far as I'm concerned, you's a goddamn cotton-picker, boy, and that's all you'll ever amount to! And as long as there's a breath in my body, I'm gonna continue to see that you remain so!"

226

"But Mr. Miles, we done paid our dues. We's been breaking our backs on your behalf for twenty some-odd years now and ain't even got a dime to show for it. So I don't think it's fair to go threatening me like this, especially after all we've been doing for you!"

My father's observations were true and somewhat effective, at least for the time being, and were awfully hard to deny. He and his family had actually been robbed of their labor and practically every vestige of dignity.

He'd never heard my father speak in such an aggressive way. So for the first time he found himself admiring my father.

'But N-A-A-A-W, on second thought, 'this nigger's bristling up to me! And as a matter of fact, he's completely out of line.' So - as a white citizen – he felt it was his solemn duty to slam Dad back into his place!

My father's unusual outburst had actually troubled the shyster's conscience, yet it served to make him all-the-more angry. So in terms of overriding his guilt, he reminded himself that my father was just a nigger - a black ass son of a bitch. So, why should he rationalize his lofty position? He was, therefore inclined to belittle my dad, make him feel as though he was lower than dirt on the ground, and did not even deserve a right to breathe.

He was old and feeble all right, but still the pride of the south - still the General Lee of the cotton plantations - and therefore had more guts than an entire stack of black sons of bitches all stacked up on top of one another, at least in his own mind he had.

So, "Boy," he shouted! "You ain't nothing but a goddamned nigger and that's all you'll ever amount to! And I suggest you watch your damn tongue when you address me! I know you been running your black ass in and out of Clarksdale, but that don't give you no right to get cocky with me. And one more thing you black motherfucker: you couldn't outsmart the dumbest of white men, let alone a swift son of a bitch like myself! I therefore, suggest you step your black ass back in line and I mean pretty goddamn quick!"

CHAPTER 56 "AN ILLOGICAL DECISION"

My father got the message, all right. And it suddenly dawned on him how manipulated he'd been. In fact, he was supposed to come a-crawling back once Mr. Merritt was finished with him. He'd provoked the altercation yet all he'd done throughout the entire ordeal was defend him self. So, Mr. Miles, as usual, had kicked him dead in the ass again. But they had vowed not to work for him again. Yet my father had to give the impression they would, He'd otherwise, never been able to get rid of him.

So, "Sorry," said my dad, "but I'm not in my right mind today."

"Now that's about the smartest thing you done said," said Mr. Miles.

"Besides, I have to run this by my wife, sir."

"Well, why didn't you say so," said the old man? "Tell Magnolia to come on out here. Hell, we can settle this matter right here and right now!"

"I'm sorry, but she's not home, sir" my Dad said. "But if you give us a week to ten days, we'll settle this matter one way or another."

"One way or another," the old man repeated, while shifting his car into gear! "Ain't but one judicious choice, boy," he said, "just one judicious choice!" Before he slammed his foot to the floor and he took off.

Back inside, my father shared the gist of the conversation with Mom who'd landed a job earning $9.50 a week at a laundry mat in Clarksdale.   I had found a job myself working on a dry cleaning truck, which paid $12.50 a week. So, knowing he wouldn't be able to find a job, my father settled on the idea of collecting scrap metal. Grady was recently inducted into the army and, as a result, Mom had an extra $72.00 a month coming. So, with such a windfall, we figured on making out like bandits in the city.

But thanks to Mr. Miles' connections, the southern bureaucrats refused to honor the allotment. So Mom wrote a letter to President Roosevelt, who responded favorably but to no avail. So they decided to move on anyway. And for the first time since falling into The Triple B Trap, we packed up and moved in broad daylight - the boldest statement my family ever made.

Yet, the move was not so easily accepted since it was such a great surprise to Mr. Merritt and Mr. Miles, who considered it a blatant expression of insanity! They wondered, 'How an unemployable Negro with twelve mouths to feed expected to survive within the city limits?' The very idea was against all logical common sense.

CHAPTER 57   "436 GRANT STREET"

Now things were much different on Grant Street. There were finally other Negro children to play with and a school merely two blocks away. The dump was approximately two miles up the road. And though we missed the activity on the railroad, there was nothing else to miss about that retched situation.

I met the laundry truck at six each morning and returned after dark. My new boss drove up to rural houses where I jumped off to deliver clean clothes or pick-up dirty ones. My duties also included tagging the clothes and tying them into separate bundles. I was otherwise an involuntary sounding board for my white boss. I worked on the truck nine months and attended school three the first year. I reversed that process the following year.

And just as promised, the entire white establishment assisted Mr. Miles in his endeavor to subdue my father. There was no work for him whatsoever. And though he often tried, he'd always return home broken down and brokenhearted.

My mother, who took a stroll downtown one day, passed Bennett's Furniture Store. The owner stopped her to divulge a startling piece of news. My brother McClain apparently owed him $52 which he'd promised to pay for the better part of a year. So chomping down on a huge black cigar, he claimed he'd went his limit.

"Tonight," he said, "me and some of Clarksdale's finest

are gonna pay that boy a visit."

Not quite knowing how to respond, my mother asked could she assume my brother's debt but he refused her. "Please," she begged. "Give me several months and I'll scrape up the entire balance."

"Hell no," shouted Bennett! "I was practically bored to death, anyhow. But thanks to that black son of a bitch, I've got something to do tonight."

"But please," begged Mom. "Give me a chance. I'll see to it that he lives up to his responsibility."

"I gave your son credit in good faith," said Bennett, "so you can beg all you want. I'm tearing into his ass tonight! I'm gonna teach him something you should've taught him long ago. By the time we finish, he won't be able to lie to no more white folks. Now that much I promise."

"But Mr. Bennett," begged Mom, pulling eleven dollars from her purse - a part of next month's rent - but he refused that as well. So she decided she'd better go home. And no sooner had she arrived, she and my father got into the car then headed off towards Memphis.

McClain had a job and was preaching in Memphis, but he lived in a cottage between Clarksdale and the Tennessee border. Dusk was falling when they arrived and hooded men surrounded the cottage, which set on a knoll surrounded by a ditch. But there were no more houses around.

No one was home when they arrived, which my parents

regarded as a blessing. The hooded men, who'd already set the ditch afire, were working themselves into a frenzy! And there was no doubt they'd burn the entire structure to the ground.

Just a few miles beyond there, my dad spotted a lone car in his rearview mirror about three quarters of a mile behind him. So after checking his gauge he continued a lawful dispatch. They finally spotted McClain approximately twelve miles up the road, he and his wife throttling towards Clarksdale in his Chevrolet convertible. Trying to warn them, my dad blew profusely as Mom frantically waved. The cops, coming up the rear, turned their siren on. Thanks to the noise and the flashing lights, McClain - who swiftly caught on - spun around and sped off towards Memphis, his wife waving back in gratitude yet the cops still in hot pursuit.

It was getting darker now and they knew they were in a volatile situation, yet they took the liberty to say silent prayers for my brother, his wife and baby. But then amid the confusion, it dawned on them how risky it was to even think of turning back. Even worse, they couldn't afford to continue their present course. The cops chasing McClain would eventually double back and boy would they be irritated, especially if they hadn't caught up with my brother. Adding to their dilemma, the men torching the house would also be awaiting their return.

There was no choice other than to keep pressing forward in hopes of running upon a crossroads. But even then, they'd have to navigate that through back wood territory and, if they were lucky, they'd reconnect on one of the main highways...but God only knew where. If they were fortunate enough to resurface on Highway 49 or 61, they could take either one back to Clarksdale. But even this was risky thinking because should something happen to the car, they'd be stuck in KKK territory with not a single soul to turn to.

Instead of pondering their own safety, Mother was concerned about McClain and hadn't considered the fact they could cross paths with the same cops pursuing him. But as luck would have it, my father ran up on a gravel road flanked by corn stalks, which he took. This led to a dirt road, which they bumped around on for what seemed like forever. He methodically worked his way back to the main highway but in some far distant place. By that time however, Bennett and his gang of thugs were probably home in bed.

CHAPTER 58   "A ROMANTIC THOUGHT"

My dad eventually pulled out on Highway 49 but he was headed in the wrong direction. After passing a sign and realizing he was en route to Mount Bayou - the only black haven in the state - he turned and headed back towards Clarksdale.

Beneath the dome of a starry night, my father's car was silhouetted by moonlight. And as he slowed to a relaxed pace, "Look," he said pointing into the sky. "That old moon...it ain't got a worry the world, does it?"

"Ooh-Wee," said Mom, tucking her hands into his. "It does look quite impressive, now don't it?" She then squeezed his hand even tighter and said, "Thanks, honey. You didn't have to do that you know, now don't you?"

"Do what," my dad said as if he didn't know what she was talking about.

"For being there for my child when he needed you. I'll never be able to thank you enough."

"Aw, come on, Magnolia. How could I let that boy down without letting you down? Don't mention it anymore, okay?

She lifted her eyes back into the heavens. "Just look - a shooting star! Look! See? There it goes, see? Now imagine that - my own shooting star. Now that must be an omen." Her eyes all a-glow now, she marveled, "It must be a sign that my child got away. I bet you anything they're somewhere in Memphis all safe and sound...probably taking in a movie!"

"And what makes you so sure?"

"I just know," said Mom. "I can feel it in my bones, that's why!"

"But how do you know you ain't miscalculating this thing," my father asked?

"I just know," assured Mom. "Haven't you ever heard of a mother's intuition?"

"So what's that?"

"Something we women use as an emotional guide."

"Oh, okay. But how do you know this ain't the one time when your 'whatchamcallit' ain't working?"

"Aw, Edmond, don't be so negative, especially when I'm trying to make a connection with the stars."

"Oh, is that so," said Daddy? "I didn't know you could do that."

"Well, now you that know," she said with a renewed twinkle.

"Well, what else is them stars telling you? Is they telling you anything about me?"

"Nope. Except that old moon up there is shining strictly for your pleasure."

"Aw, Magnolia, that thing ain't shinning for me, it's shining for the whole wide world to see!"

They'd both begun engaging in romantic thought which prompted him to reach over and turn the radio on. But the speakers, which were usually warm and deep, produced such an obnoxious disturbance!

"Oh, no," shouted Mom! "Turn that thing off! Please, turn it off!"

So, frantically, my father struggled through the knobs and eventually turned the thing off.

"Why," asked my mom, "did you do that at this particular time?"

"I don't know," said Dad. "I was just looking for something to, to... you know... to turn you on."

"I don't need no ole' radio to turn me on. This here is all I need."

"And just what is that?"

"*This* - just sitting next to you getting fired up by these moonbeams. That'll do it every time."

"Oh! Is that so?"

"Just about every time," she said!

"Well, alright," said Dad! "Now don't you start no mess, Magnolia, and there won't be none! What's come over you anyhow? You forgetting we got all them children waiting for us?"

238

"Aw Honey, that's the point. They're at home and we're out here in the boondocks! And these moonbeams are giving me such a warm sensation. Them kids can wait! They're probably in bed asleep, anyhow."

"And the way you carrying on, looks like I'm gonna have to rock you to sleep, as well."

"That's just fine with me!"

"Watch out now! What's come over you anyhow?"

"Must be moon madness..."

"Whatever it is, it done sure cast a spell over you tonight. I suggest you get a hold of yourself before we be done-done something rash and you end up all knocked up again!"

"I kinda feel like I did when we first got married, Edmond, especially since I have a distinct feeling my son's gonna be alright. But I doubt if you remember."

"Oh, I remember it all right. We were carrying on like something scandalous there for awhile, weren't we?"

"Ooh, baby, we certainly were, weren't we? And from the way I feel now, we can start the process all over again."

"Well, now Magnolia, I know how you feel," he said, squeezing her even tighter. "But I ain't comfortable with it, okay? Let's just wait till we get home, okay?"

"But why pass up such an opportunity?"

"I ain't passed up nothing Magnolia! All I said was let's wait till we get home."

"I know," she said, staring into the distance. "But that's okay. I love you anyway."

"O-o-o-o-h w-e-e-e! Now keep that up," he said in response to her rubbing the back of his neck, "I *guarantee you, you* won't be disappointed tonight, baby! And by the time I get you home, it's gonna be on!"

They sat there listening to the roar of my father's engine after which he threw his hand out the window and allowed the wind to penetrate his fingers. They eventually rode through Tut Wiley then Rucks and through Mattson then finally, into the Clarksdale city limits.

CHAPTER 59   "THE FIRST RIDE ON THE LAST TRAIN"

Three days later, Mom received a letter from McClain who, since he'd lost practically everything he owned, expressed his sadness. He bragged, however, about out running the cops but complained of his inability to visit with the family again. Ironically, though, he said they made it just in time to catch a movie.

There were other obstacles, most of which the family was able to overcome until the Junk King decided he couldn't do business with my father anymore. Several weeks later, a white boy on a bicycle ran over James Lee on the sidewalk. He beat the boy up and consequently left town on the first thing smoking. As it turned out, he had to leave his wife and 1 year-old baby behind...a sad day. But he eventually learned that his wife had been sexually involved with her white boss. So, once again, the white man killed two birds with a single stone.

Mr. Miles, meanwhile, continued his never-ending quest to subdue my father, which was no secret. Yet my father was in denial. Mom, she saw the writing on the wall. She wanted to get out of the situation before it collapsed completely. And, though quite reluctantly, my father eventually became more interested in California. But as usual, he was afraid of change. He'd been entrapped in The Triple B System so long now until he actually couldn't imagine much of anything different. Mom, who'd already been to California, knew it was a better place especially before Ronald Reagan became

Governor. But dad needed a jolt of which she was more than willing to provide. But being that he was stubborn, she knew she had to strike fast, hard and precise. So she came home from work one day, just as furious as could be.

"Edmond Wright," she said slamming the door behind her. "You and these boys can stay here as long as you want to. But my girls and me, we're getting out of here as fast as we can!"

"So what's the problem," asked Dad taken totally by surprise?

"What's the problem," bellowed Mom? "Them dogs out there followed me all the way home. Talking about me all up under my clothes. They're the problem! You're the problem! And everybody and everything in this dog-infested town is the problem! That's what's the problem," she said, packing her suitcase!

Dad rushed to the window and pulled the curtains aside. He saw the two cops who'd went to the nearest corner and turned around and were headed back towards Fourth Street. The one riding shotgun had his cap pulled down over his eyes and was grinning, pretending he was ashamed, which he clearly wasn't. My father felt a sudden rush of anger but what he could do? They'd long since itched to do him in but only to the point he'd remain able to work a patch of cotton.

Mom wasted no time, though. She immediately wired Inez who, within days, sent her six one-way tickets.

So she and the five remaining girls boarded the train, leaving my dad and me and my two younger brothers, who promised to join them as soon as possible – which, at that time, I was not so sure of?

My dad had to take responsibility now - for himself and for the remaining boys - or perish. So he started liquidating his personal belongings, of which he didn't have much worthy of selling. Yet, he had a personal attachment to practically everything he owned, especially the 1946 Pontiac, which was his greatest asset. He actually didn't want to part with it and probably wouldn't have if Mama hadn't, took such a strong initiative. Yet he ended up selling it to a fast-talking shyster for less than half the car's value.

An entire month later, he was still trying to raise enough money to make it to California. Practically all his life, he'd never known anything but how to work a patch of cotton. So, salesmanship was not his forte'. He'd actually sold nothing except the car he sold Leo, and even then he was taken. As long as he could remember, he'd traded at the country store, raised hogs, chickens and cows, grew turnip greens and practically everything else his family consumed. He had a limited knowledge of money, so the art of dealership was not one of his greatest attributes. The only time he'd got his hands on a decent piece, he squandered it right away.

Mom, at long last, wired him every cent she hadn't spent. So this, coupled with his meager profits, gave him the edge he needed. Yet he grappled with not being able to sell everything he owned - an old stove, a hand held

243

saw, a meat grinder, and an out of date dinette set. Yet realizing he'd have to sell the junk or leave it, he decided he'd cut his losses and run.

As we walked the length of the train towards the last car, our father, my two brothers and I couldn't help but notice the lively chatter among passengers. And while mini spurts of steam provided ambiance, we took our seats in the last car.

Then, slightly before dusk, the train pulled out leaving a trail of smoke against the southern hemisphere. Seated next to a window on the left, I was determined to scan every bit of territory between Clarksdale and the California state line. And one of the first things I saw was our old house at the edge of the dump where, just like Frankie D. and me, two little raggedy boys waved at the passing train. I was happy to know I'd never have to review that sight again. So, picking up speed, we passed the water tower, then the sawmill at Lyons, and off into the wide-open spaces.

We were soon chasing the mighty Mississippi until we crossed a trestle, which took us from her shores. From there, all I could see were lighted windows of isolated homes, most of which I had ran up on their porches to pick-up dirty clothes. I had no way of knowing that within an hour, the train would brake for the Memphis station.

Having no idea of what he was in for, my father was reluctant to spend his last few dollars. So thank God for our Aunt Nancy who fixed us a single meal each of fried chicken, white bread and a medium-sized yam, which

244

we'd all but finished by nine thirty the next day. Beyond that, we practically starved until the third day when he finally broke down and took us into the dining car where we enjoyed the only other meal of the journey.

And as we exited the train at Union Station, I reflected on the moment we switched trains in Memphis. The last car, which we boarded in Clarksdale, was strictly for Negros. Yet when we boarded a different train in Memphis, my father took us to the rear car but it was practically filled with white folks! So we went back to the next car and then to the car beyond that.

Eventually, he ran into a porter and asked, "Where is the colored folk suppose to sit on this contraption?"

The porter released a pearly-toothed smile and said, "Just about any place you want to on this train, sir!"

Baffled, my father didn't know what to do! He turned and went back to the rear car and then the front car again, back to the rear car - back and forth like an out of control robot. He finally stopped in the second car just long enough to wipe his brow.

"Y'all go on and sit down," he said. "Just take them seats right there." Then, with eyes darting back and forth as if he'd stole something, he took the seat behind us.

I couldn't help but notice how some people were snickering at my dad, which I may have done had I not been so closely related. But as far as I was concerned, those who did, instead, should've felt honored. For whether they knew it or not, they were witnessing 50 years of hard-core programming at the precise moment it began to unravel.

And, 'What,' I wondered, 'were the chances they'd ever observe such a phenomenon again?' And, most importantly, did they know they were witnessing a genuine slice of American history in the making which, in their wildest dreams, they'd never be able to comprehend the full extent of its inert ingredients?'

Now I heard it rarely rained in Southern California. Yet as we emerged from Union Station, it was raining cats and dogs! And for an entire week, it continued to pour like a never-ending waterfall.

But then one day, the sun burst through! And for the first time ever, Frankie D. and I were proud students at Vermont Avenue Elementary School, which, during pre-Reagan years, was totally integrated.

I personally felt as though I'd been transported to another planet and given a brand new lease on life. And, oh, what a wonderful, wonderful beginning!

-THE BEGINNING-

Made in the USA
San Bernardino, CA
26 August 2017